Life Starts When The Church Ends

-The Chronicles of Bird-

Sherrad O'Neil Glosson

ISBN-13: 978-0-692-57980-0

Editor Dr. Frances Curtis-Fields

Co-editor Jackie Roman

Book cover design by @kingray_ent

ACKNOWLEDGMENTS

It's Friday, November 13, 2015 at 1:34pm and I'm sitting on my mom's couch tryna' send this book in for print. So if I miss a name just know that I'm rushing to get this book out for ya'll to read this awesome story, ya dig! Say word! Sho you're right!! Lol excuse that last part. I'm just drawing a blank..

I want to thank God for blessing me with the gift of creativity and the ability to put it on paper. Special thanks to my parents Pastor Darryl and 1st Lady Angelique Spires, my grandparents Josie Williams and the late Reverend Hezekiah Williams R.I.H, grandparents Mr. John & Kathy Spires, my aunts, uncles, cousins, friends, friends of friends. Thanks to my cousin Demetrius Solomon for allowing me to use your son Tyler Solomon a.k.a Tank for the cover. Thanks for reading Brandy and Renita. Make sure ya'll check out Renita's new business venture info@hashtagaddictedtojesus.com for more info. You can find her on facebook and Instagram @Hashtagaddictedtojesus The people who helped edit, Jackie Roman, and Dr. Frances "Ricky" Curtis-Fields and all my dance family. Most importantly thank you to all of you that believe in me. R.I.P. Michigan Mike. To all my brothers and sisters incarcerated. Remember, I was there too. Keep ya head up!

PROLOGUE

"Man, it's two thirty in the morning already?"

"Yeah, you're the one that wanted to stay over there all day."

My friends and I had just left from this Fourth of July party over on Six Mile and Greenfield. There's a park over on Forrer and Prevost cross streets that the people in the hood put together. There were all kinds of fireworks, basketball tournaments, and just some good ole community fun. Local artists from the city came by to give us their "Hot 16," blessing the crowds with their lyrical content, and everybody was just chillin', drankin', smokin', and having a good time enjoying the festivities in the hood. There were no worries about anybody getting hurt or the police shutting anything down. It's what we called the "Black People Heaven" for the moment. Just living our version of Heaven as if it were our last time here on Earth.

Those were the kind of days that used to take place back in the day before the crack era hit the city. Detroit was of the most "happening" places. It was a place where singers were made, some of the fanciest cars were driven, and a place where the dance life was at an all-time high. Since the new millennium hit, Detroit now is nothing but a city of drug dealers and some of the most heartless boys and girls you could ever meet. When the mayor showed people that even a status couldn't take the hood out of you, people just started living a life without any hope or dreams.

We left a few minutes ago and rode down Grand River looking for a place to get something to eat. When you get a lil bit of drugs and alcohol in your system the body immediately craves for food and good sweets to fulfill its desire. I'm having Grade-A munchies but it's late and everything I'm driving past is closed. I saw that Coney Island was open, but don't feel like waiting on them to cook the food. I really need instant gratification but sometimes stopping at a Coney at this time of night isn't always the best idea. Even the Coney Island restaurants in the suburbs close before 11 at night.

"Let's go to McDonald's," my home girl Gooney yelled from the back seat.

"Nah man, I'm tired of eating at McDonald's. We eat there every time we get high."

She replied. "Yeah, that's because they have a dollar menu."

I busted out laughing. "One of my homeboys from school works down at the White Castle on Lahser Road. He told me he'd be working tonight, and besides, McDonald's food is not even real meat I heard. Their food never get old, it just sits there looking like hard plastic."

"So your boy is gonna' hook us up, right?" Gooney asked.

"He betta, Buck chimed in from the passenger seat. "I'm hungry as hell right now," Buck rubbed his stomach as he heard it growling.

"I'm telling you!" Gooney said.

I pulled up to White Castle and the line was wrapped around the building as usual, for a night like this.

"Is the inside open?" said Gooney.

I looked, but didn't see anyone on the inside. I parked the car anyway. As hungry as I am I hope I don't have to sit in this line all night.

"Are y'all coming in with me?"

"Nah man, I'm too damn high to even walk right now. Hell, I can barely think for myself at this point, but I will take a crave case though," Buck replied, in a low voice with eyes halfway open.

"Gooney, you comin' with me?" I said, waiting for a response. "Gooney?" I looked in the back seat and she was acting like she was sleep.

"Man, y'all lazy as hell." I slammed the door after I got out the car.

"Aye, Bird, get me a cherry slushy too." Gooney yelled, as I was halfway to the door.

"Yea ok, whatever!" I shouted back.

I opened the door, and my homeboy from school was on the grill cooking some burgers.

"Hey, we closed man. I just forgot to lock the door," he said in response to the bell that went off. He didn't even look up.

"Aye-Yo, Tee, it's me," I yelled over the counter.

He looked up, "oh, what's up, Bird? What's good, Homie?"

"Trying to get right. What's up?"

"Man, we are running slow as hell tonight. Two people called in sick today. So it's just me and Big Heavy till someone else comes in to work. They got me working like a slave in here."

"I see," I said, looking out the window at the long line of cars outside, "That's why I came on the inside."

Someone tapped on the drive thru window screaming "How long is it gon' be on them burgers, Cuz?" I've been out here for fifteen minutes?"

"Yeah, we usually lock the door after a certain time, but I've been so damn busy I just forgot. We all outta' order in here man, but what do you need?"

"Man, I need a crave case."

"THIRTY BURGERS! Man, you must be high?"

We both bursted out laughing.

"Man, I'm so zooted right now, and I got the crew with me."

"They outside in the car stuck, huh?"

"You know they're actin' like they can't move. Gooney acted like she was sleep just so she wouldn't have to come in."

"Aight', well look, you know it's gon' take me a minute because of the line. Gimme' about twenty minutes."

"Aight,' man, take yo' time. Grab me a grape slushy real quick though."

My phone went off and when I looked at the caller, it was my mom. I'm too high to even answer it so I sent her call to voicemail.

She sent me a text telling me to make sure I drive safe and watch out for people driving drunk.

Seconds later, Tee came back with my drink, then went back to help Big Hev make the orders.

The door opened up, and I turned around.

Standing there was a dark-skinned guy with braids, wearing sunglasses dressed in an all black Dickie outfit. A true Detroit hookup. I looked at him, and then looked away. He looked kind of familiar, but when you buzzed, everybody looks like somebody.

"Aye, man, I think they closed," I said looking back at him.

" Bird?" He said.

"Who is you?" I replied back reaching for my gun but realized I left it in the car.

"It's me, Tom Tom!" He said as he took his glasses off.

"Tom t—oh, what's up baby? When you get out?"

"I just got out this morning. You know they can't hold somebody like me down for long."

Tom Tom and I were in county jail together. I was only there for fighting, but he on the other hand, was facing a murder case at the age of twelve.

"Good to see you, man. It's been a long time, Homie. I see you been hittin' them weights."

"Oh yeah, he said flexing every muscle. You know I had to go hard in the paint. That was all I could do." He said looking toward the back where Hev and Tee were cooking and making orders. Aye look, it was good to see you, Homie, straight up," He said as we gave each other five, and a half shoulder hug. Then he headed out the door.

"You ain't gon' get nothing to eat? My boy, Tee, will hook you up if you hungry?" I asked him.

"Nah, Homie, I got something else on the floor," He replied and then he left.

"Aye, Bird," Tee yelled five minutes later. "Here you go, Homie." He came up to the counter with the food.

"Good lookin' out, man. I'm starving." I grabbed the bag and headed to the door until I remembered I needed to get a cherry slushy for Gooney.

"Aye, Tee, I need another slushy, a cherry one."

"Aight, hold up." He went to make the slushy.

The door opened up and I turned around. There was someone wearing a black mask, holding a pistol in his hand. He headed straight to the counter and pointed the pistol at Tee.

He yelled, "GIMMIE ALL THE MONEY, CUZ! RIGHT NOW!"

"Tom, Tom," I yelled as I stood there in shock, hoping I was not in line to get shot. I stood there, shaking like a dope fiend needing a fix.

"HURRY UP!" He yelled again, with the pistol still pointing at Tee cocking the hammer back. I just knew he was about to pull the trigger. Tee was moving as fast as he could, and so was Hev.

I'm in no position to try and be a hero. I just hope Tom-Tom wouldn't kill them. In the back of my mind I was wondering if Gooney or Buck could see what was going on from the car.

"HURRY THE HELL UP!" Tom Tom yelled again.

BLAYAH! BLAYAH!

Tom Tom let off two shots, and I dropped the slushy on the ground. Tee and Hev each caught a bullet to the chest and flew back. Blood splattered on the counter and on the grill. I just stood there, not wanting to make any sudden moves. Tom Tom jumped over the counter and went straight to the cash register taking all the money. I just stood there as he went to the back of the place and came back with the videotape in his hand.

He jumped back over the counter and looked me straight in my eyes. For a second I thought he was about to shoot me, but he put his mask on and ran out the door. As paranoid as I was, I just stood there, stuck in a trance, trying to gather my thoughts on what I just witnessed. My high was completely gone. I snapped out of it fast and ran back out to the car.

"Man, we just got robbed!" Buck yelled with a bloody nose, holding his head back trying to stop the blood from pouring down his face.

"What? By who?"

"Someone in all black. He walked up to the car and held us at gunpoint. Another guy was with him and was smacking Gooney."

I looked in the back seat, and the right side of Gooney's face was red. She was lying down holding her face as tears were coming down her cheeks.

"I tried to stop him and we started fighting. He broke my nose, and then took all my money and the gun from under the seat. That's when we heard shooting moments later in the building."

"I know, man. I just saw two people get murdered."

"What?"

"Yeah, man, and he took the tape."

I looked down at the floor and saw my gun. "I thought you said he took my gun," I said with a baffled look on my face.

"He did, and after we heard the shots he came and threw it back in the car," said Buck.

I picked it up, checked the clip, and saw that the bullets were missing.

"Don't tell me?" Gooney chimed in.

"Yeah, this fool used my gun."

"You know who it was?" said Buck.

I remained silent.

"Hurry up, let's go before the police come," Buck said, but it was already too late because the police station is down the street, and we could hear the sirens from less than a mile away.

I hopped in the car and turned the ignition, and it wouldn't start.

"Damn this car, man." I said frustrated, because if there was a time that I needed my car to start, the time is definitely now.

I turned the ignition again, and it was the same response.

"Come on, Bird, hurry up!" Gooney panicked.

"I'm trying , I'm trying." I looked towards the street and I could see the lights glaring in the night sky.

"Bird, Come on!" Buck yelled from outside the car with the door open.

"The police are coming!" Gooney yelled, as I was tryna get the car started .

"WAIT!" I yelled, as they both took off running, and seconds later, four squad cars swooped up on me, and they jumped out the cars with their rifles pointed.

"DON'T MOVE! I swear if you move, I will shoot you till you die, and come back to life." An officer yelled as they approached my car, "Put your hands up where I can see them."

I dropped the gun to the ground and put my hands in the air. My heart was beating a thousand miles an hour, and from the looks of it, it don't look like it's gonna' get any better.

"Don't look at me; keep your eyes on the wheel. Now, slowly take your right hand and open the door from the outside. Any sudden movement and we're gonna' take this to the next level," he warned.

I reached outside the car.

"Easy," he said, as I opened the door.

"There are two down behind the counter." One of the officers said coming from inside the building.

I stepped out with my hands shaking in the air, "I didn't do anything, sir!" I pleaded.

"QUIET! I didn't ask you to talk did I?"

As soon as my feet touched the concrete two of the cops came, threw me to the ground face down, and immediately slapped the cuffs on me. Cuffing my hands behind my back, and cuffing my ankles behind me. I was hog-tied.

I thought to myself "This can't possibly be happening to me right now."

They tossed me into the back of a squad car belly down.

The officers were talking amongst themselves, and then moments later, one of them sat in the front seat.

"Two bodies, a robbery, and a possible murder weapon? You've got to be one of the dumbest criminals of all time, son. You are going down tonight buddy." He said with a smile.

I looked out the window and saw the police talking to some of the people that remained after the shooting occurred, and the Channel 2 news just pulled up. The camera man jumped out the van before it could even stop moving, and rushed over to the car putting the camera in my face.I kept my head low as the officer pulled off and headed downtown to police headquarters at 1300 Beaubien.

"Let me get my phone call," I asked in anger as they dragged me through the back door of the station. They acted like they didn't hear a word that came outta' my mouth.

I tried to shake loose from them as they threw me into the bull-pin with the other inmates.

I looked around and there had to be about sixty other people in this little cell, and only one phone. Most of them looked like they were excessively drunk and too far gone to even be on the streets. Some of them looked like straight convicts, and others look like crack heads standing in the corner scratching their arms. It was complete chaos, and the complete opposite of how I was actually supposed to spend my eighteenth birthday.

I was next in line for the phone, and I would have been on it, but the person in front of me was on his third call. I know he's gotten through on all his calls, and I know damn well he knows that I've been waiting to use the phone as well. Every time he hung up, he dialed another number then looks at me smiling.

"Aye, man, can I use the phone?" I asked with the utmost respect, but the big white guy ignored me.

I tapped him on his shoulder, "Aye, man."

"What the hell is the problem, boy?" he yelled

"I just wanna' use the phone, man. I know you got through already."

"You'll use the phone when I'm done. Now, back off."

"WHAT?"

"You heard me," He said and turned around and started talking back on the phone. I looked around the cell, and all the attention was on me. I waited a few seconds, and then took a swing. I caught him behind the right side of his ear, and he fell forward.

He got up and grabbed me and threw me into the wall, and punched me twice in the ribs. The inmates started getting riled up. As soon as I backed up from the blows he gave, I caught my breath, and caught him with a punch in his mouth. I didn't waste any time after that. I scooped him up off the ground and he was tryna' to pound me on my back, but I didn't give him a chance. I dropped him on the back of his head and knocked him out.

All the inmates looked at me and there was complete silence. I stood up, backed up to the wall, and went to the phone to make my long awaited call.

"Curtis, this better be you, Boy, what in the h.."

"Ma, I swear I didn't do anything."

"I told you about hangin' in them streets with them gangs. Didn't I tell you, you were gonna' be either locked up or dead? Now look at you."

"I told him the same thing," I heard my cousin in the back and then he picked up the phone.

"Tim, I swear, bro."

"Naw, it's too late for that, cuzzo. You put yourself in this situation, now you figure it out!"

"Hello….HELLO!!!!!" They hung up the phone.

Isn't that something? My mom don't believe me or want anything to do with me, and my cousin Tim went from telling me about how real the streets are and how I need to adapt to the way things are to telling me that I'm pretty much on my own. People are real quick to tell you how to run the streets, how to sell dope, or shoot a pistol, but have nothing to say on how to get out of a tight situation.

But like my uncle Charlie used to tell me, "Life starts when the church ends." I've yet to crack the atom on what he meant by that because he's been saying that to me ever since I was a little kid. I guess that's something I'll learn as I get older, and what better time to think about getting older than right now. Let me take you back a few years and tell you how this happened. "Aye, officer, I need some paper and a pencil." I gotta tell people about this.

Life Starts When The Church Ends

CHAPTER 1

EIGHT YEARS EARLIER

My mom and I just moved to Detroit, Michigan about two months ago, before the summer started, from Dubach, Louisiana. It's a vast difference between down south and up north. The biggest of them all is the weather. Down south it's extremely hot in the summer and the bugs are about the size of small dogs crawling around everywhere.

You can tell that it's a completely different culture here and it's been a major culture shock for me as well as for my mom. She went back and forth from up north to down south as a kid, but when the crack era hit in Detroit and Generation X was beginning to form, she decided that she didn't want me to end up like the rest of the kids coming of age. Down south it could get up to a hundred degrees easy, but at night it can be just as cold as the mid-winter on an Alaskan night. The people in the South are really friendly though. My mom tells me there's nothing like southern hospitality. Here in Detroit though, it's pretty much in the 80's and 90's most of the time.

What's really cool about it is when this happens, a big truck with a swimming pool full of water comes to the neighborhood and all the kids jump in to cool off. Sometimes when there was no Swim-mobile, as they called it, the rebels of the neighborhood would pop the caps off the fire hydrants and we would run through the outpour until one of the neighbors complained about their basement flooding or at least that would be the reason they tell us.

My mom and her boyfriend were always having issues and she got to the point where she couldn't take it anymore. Most of the time it was when he would come home at night from a bar and pick fights with her about why she always came home from work late. He always accused her of sleeping with other men and he would be so drunk that he would forget that she worked a full time job helping out at the local schools, and a part time job waiting tables on top of that. All he did was sit around the house and watch TV collecting unemployment because he had a smoking problem. He would stop smoking just long enough to get a job and find every reason to get himself fired.

As crazy as that may sound, I guess my mom loved him that much just to let him do whatever he wanted to do. He would sometimes smack her around the room, punch her in the face, and leave all kinds of marks on her body. She would often cake a ton of makeup on her face and arms just so the people at work wouldn't be able to see the scars he left on her.

I remember being in my bedroom with the door cracked watching as he would raise his hands to her and try to make her submit to his will, and more times than not, she would. One time he told me to go outside and sit on the porch, gave me a pop sickle, and told me not to come in until I was finished. It was nearly midnight, and I was outside all alone listening to the voice of my mom echoing through the windows as the whole house would ache in pain. It never occurred to me that this wasn't normal activity because I'd seen it so much. I began to think that this was the way that a man was supposed to run his household.

I would just sit there on the porch eating my popsicle in the middle of the night. I bet I was the only kid on a school night sitting outside like that. At times, I would begin to weep as the cold air would turn my cheeks purple.

This one particular time I was tired of hearing the awful noises coming from my mom's vocal cords as if she was singing soprano in a Chicago mass choir. I threw my popsicle down, went into the backyard and grabbed my baseball bat. I went into the house and he had my mom pinned down on her back and was forcefully holding her arms over her head.

"GET OFF MEEEE!!!!!" she yelled to the top of her lungs. She would begin to choke and cough from screaming that was torturing her lungs.

I took the bat with both hands and held it over my head and swung it downward as hard as I could across the top of his head. He fell over to his side, holding his head, and yelling in pain. My mom grabbed me and hugged me crying and screaming, but he was so drunk that he acted like it barely fazed him. The blood from his head ran out like a river and I realized I swung with some power that I didn't know I had.

He just got up and left. My mom told me to pack my things because we were leaving. I didn't understand what that meant because I didn't know where we could possibly be going. She packed up almost every item of clothing we had and then I knew that we were going to be gone for a long time. We took a cab to the Greyhound station and headed to Detroit.

I was actually born in Detroit, and raised in the projects. This is where most of my family lives. It felt good to be back with my grandparents. My grandmother moved up here back in the day when the "Big Three" was booming. Now, she runs a church over in Highland Park called Kingdom of the True and Living God Baptist Church. We began to attend after we came back to town. Well, not so much my mom, she comes to church when she feels like it. She and her cousins always go to this nightclub called Legends over on Telegraph and Schoolcraft. They drink and party so much that when they wake up on Sunday morning they are still "slizzard" as my cousin would say, from the night before.

My grandmother on the other hand would make sure that my cousins and I were in church every Sunday. We couldn't seem to miss a Sunday even if we used the greatest excuse in the world-which was 'my stomach hurts'!! My grandmother would say come to church and let the good Lord heal you. I would also try to use "all my clothes are dirty" and she would come back with—"well, put on this sheet and wrap it around your body, and we gon' call you 'Peter' today." It has been a pretty rough time since I've been up here to say the least.

My mom must not have gone out last night because she brought me to church this time. We've been here since Sunday school started, and I'm ready to go already. My grandma makes sure that I'm active every Sunday doing something, because most of the time I'm laid out on a pew counting sheep. She put me in the choir, and I don't even know how to sing. She told me that when it comes to singing for the Lord it doesn't matter what you sound like. Yeah, we'll see about that when I get to heaven. I'm pretty sure I could tick the angels off pretty good. I love sitting behind the pulpit though because I can see everything.

Like, for instance, my older cousin is about to come in at any minute and sit in the last row of the church. He always happens to be the last person to come in and the first person to leave. He always wear the same cologne, too, and it don't even smell good. It smells like dead grass if you ask me, and not to mention he always has his sunglasses on, and the sun is nowhere in sight. As soon as church is over, he runs to his truck and three minutes later it'll be smoke coming from everywhere. I even asked him about it too because I was curious, and he told me that his engine was bad, and that he needed an oil change. I guess he needs one every week because every Sunday it's the same thing.

Oh, and look at this here. These same two women keep walking up and down the street. Back and forth, back and forth from one car to another. One woman will be missing for a few minutes and then next thing I know, she's back, and then the other woman is gone. They must have a lot of friends because they hop in and out of cars left and right, not to mention the fish net stockings they are wearing. A different color every week even when It's 90 degrees outside. I just laugh at how different Detroit is compared to the South.

The liquor store just opened up, and sure enough there's a line of these ole' raggedy looking folk waiting to get into the store. They've been out there for at least an hour or two. I wonder why they've got two liquor stores right across from each other . I notice up here in Detroit that there is either a church, or a liquor store on every corner. People are waiting to get in like they must have a special on potato chips. Funny, I know, but it's just one of the things I've noticed. My grandmother tells me that I'm very observant.

I just heard my grandfather say something about Jesus turning water into wine, and I'm looking at the sign on the store across the street that reads, "Beer and Wine," and I'm thinking, maybe people up here have their own way of following Jesus. Maybe they don't need His assistance when it comes to the wine. I'm guessing the little cup of wine and the little cracker that they give in church is not enough so they get their own bottle, and box of cheese nips and bring them to church with them. I mean, Jesus turned water to wine, so I guess it's not a big deal. Who knows, this is just what I see just by staring out the windows of the church.

Church is just about over and I hope that my mom don't want to stay for dinner. I want to go home and play with my new friends that I met when I came here.

"Did you enjoy service, grandson?" my grandmother always seemed to give me a quiz afterwards to see if I was paying attention during the service. I always made sure that I caught at least one thing she said so I can repeat it to her; a classic move of mine.

"Oh yes, grandma, it was a service like no other" I said smiling.

"Oh yeah, well, what did you learn?"

"Um...I.... learned that Jesus turned water into wine, and people are at the store across the street showing him thanks as we speak." I smiled and she gave me a look that only a grandmother could give saying, "boy you better not say another word." And she gave me a kiss on the cheek.

"Graaaannndma" I moaned as she did that. She always seemed to leave her lipstick on me.

"Hey Lilyan, glad you could make it to service. You must've had an easy night huh?"

"Yeah, we didn't do too much last night."

"Y'all staying for dinner?"

I'm hoping my mom says no.

"Ahhh nah, I cooked a lil something at home."

"Yesss!" I chimed in.

"Boy, shut up." My mom shoved me

"Okay, well, I'll see you next Sunday?"

"I don't know about all that, ma, but I'll let you know alright?"

"I was talking to Curtis."

"Yeah, grandma I know you are coming to pick me up."

"Okay, baby, give me a hug."

She tried to hug and kiss me again, but I ran away from her. "Mom, let's go!" I yelled through the church heading to the door.

As soon as I got outside, my cousin's car was smoking like crazy again.

"Ma, look. Tim needs an oil change again."

She started laughing "boy, what?"

"Cousin Tim said that his car be smoking so much because he needs an oil change."

She started laughing again as if I was telling a joke that even I couldn't grasp.

Tim honked his horn twice as we were on our way to the car.

"He know he's a mess." My mom started shaking her head.

We got in the car and headed home.

We stay out in Ecorse, Michigan, which is near the southwest side of Detroit, in the projects on 4th Street. We got home in no time and when we pulled up to the curb, my neighbor was sitting on the porch. We call him Uncle Charlie, and let me tell you a little something about him.

Uncle Charlie lived in the projects longer than anyone over here, and from what I've seen, he's the most respected too.

Better believe that if anything goes down in the neighborhood, he knows about it, and will take matters into his own two hands. He's about five feet tall with a Jerri curl in his hair in which he keeps mad activator in at all times. Don't let the sun be out. His hair will be glistening from afar like he has little diamonds in his head. He wears the most colorful clothing and keeps at least two women with him at all times. I even saw some lady feeding him grapes while the other was doing his nails.

I really don't understand it, but that's him I guess, to each his own, but he's cool. I like talking to him because he gives me the best pep talks I've ever had from a man. I feel like he's my real uncle at times. Occasionally, he will drop a jewel as he calls it and it would take days for me to figure out what he really meant by it. Lately, he's been saying this same line that I still don't quite understand.

"Wassup, Young Buck? He said as I was getting out of the car.

"What's up, uncle Charlie?"

"I see you coming from church again?"

"Yeah, you know how it is. I have to go every Sunday."

"Ain't nothing wrong with that."

"Yeah, I guess not." But I was waiting on him to say…..

"Young Buck." He yelled as I was seconds away from walking in the house.

"Uh huh."

"You know life starts when the church ends don't cha?"

I knew it was coming, and I've yet to know what that means. I guess it's one of those old people quotes that I'll get when I'm older, or at least that's what he tells me.

"Yeah, I know…I know." I yelled back with a confused look on my face as usual.

"Hey, Charlie." My mom said before going in the house.

"Hey dere gale." He yelled back.

"Hey, what's up Curtis?" the girl from next door yelled.

"What's up, Gooney?"

"You coming outside?"

"Yeah, as soon as I change my clothes; I'll be out."

"He'll be out as soon as he cleans his room." My mom yelled from inside embarrassing me.

Gooney started laughing. I quickly ran inside, cleaned my room and ran by my mom as fast I could.

When I came back outside, Gooney was sitting on her porch drinking a quarter juice and playing with her yoyo.

Gooney is this cutie that I immediately met when I first moved up here. All the boys in the projects had a crush on her. She's was only eleven years old, but her body was that of a high school girl. She's a bit of a tomboy though, and she loves to play sports. Ever since we've met, it's been a tight friendship.

"Hey, Curtis, how was church?"

"Church was church. Lemme get some," I tried to grab her juice outta her hand.

"Nawl, boy move," She backed up, squirting some on me.

"Oh, no you didn't," I uttered.

"What's up, y'all?" we turned around and it was Buck riding up on his ten speed.

Buck is white, but you would think he was black if you closed your eyes and listened to him talk. Probably because three out of four of his brothers are of African descent. He got the name Buck because he likes to fight. His brothers were always trying to make him tough because he looks like a nerd with blonde braids and glasses. So much for looking smart nowadays.

"What's up, Buck?"

"What's up, Curtis, where you coming from, Church?"

"You know it!"

"Man, you stay at church."

"Look at Charlie," Gooney pointed. He keeps a house full of women. I wonder what they doing in there."

"Who knows..."I replied.

Most of the kids in the neighborhood know me as the kid from down south. I guess I didn't have enough street credibility because really, I was actually born in Detroit.

When I first moved back here, my mom would send me to the In 'N Out store to get her a Faygo red pop and some cigarettes, and on the way back there was two guys a 'lil older than me trying to bully me. They would be pushing me around and smacking me upside my head and calling me 'church boy' and all sorts of other names like 'lil country boy' and 'country grammar.' Every time my mom would send me I always knew what to look forward to either on the way there or coming back home. One time, my mom sent me to the store like usual, and I was ready for them more than they were for me.

"Curtis, I need you to go to the store for me."

"Okay."

"The money is on the table."

I grabbed the money and headed down the street to the store. I spotted the two bullies sitting on the porch, and as soon as they saw me they hurried to meet me across my path.

"Hey, there, church boy. Where you headed?"

I didn't respond. I just looked at them. One of them tried to grab my shoulder and slam me on the ground but I moved out of his way. The other one pushed me, and that's when I pulled out a five inch pocket knife that had a blade sharp enough to cut down a tree.

"Back up!" I yelled as I swung the blade at them.

"Wait! Hold on. What are you doing, church boy?" one of them yelled trying hard to get out of the way.

They both were pretty big teenagers, and I'm only a hundred pounds soaking wet, but the blade in my hand made me feel like I was much bigger.

I yelled, "from now on, y'all gonna' leave me alone, or the next time it's going to be a problem."

They backed up and walked backwards facing me and the knife the whole time making their way back to the porch.

I was huffing and puffing, scared to death as I ran back home and that's when I met Mike and Ike.

They were sitting on the porch playing Connect Four and watching me the whole time little did I know.

"Aye, yo' name Curtis?" one of them yelled.

"Yeah."

"Aye, come up here with us," They both suggested. We saw what happened down there. They've been bullying us all the time too. I'm Mike, and this is my brother Ike."

"What made you do that?" Ike chimed in.

"I was just tired of them I guess."

"Man, you showed them. Now, they not gonna' ever mess with you again after that."

"I hope not." I said in disbelief. This could just mean that I graduated from one set of problems to another.

What was so funny about Mike and Ike was that their parents named them after a box of candy, and the neighborhood knew it, and would make fun of them from time to time. They were twins. Both were light skin, and they both had green eyes. Pretty boys if you ask me, and soft as a piece Charmin tissue. I mean, I was soft too, but after they saw me pull out that knife, I was tough as nails.

It was kind of ironic to me that Gooney, Buck, Mike, and Ike's birthdays were within the months of June and July. We all celebrated at the same time, and that's how I met a lot of people in the projects when I moved here. We hung out together ever since we met. I considered them to be the brothers and sisters that I never had and they treated me like family as well. Ever since I pulled that knife out on the neighborhood bullies, they felt like I would be the one to protect us. So, since then, I kept it with me at all times.

Life Starts When The Church Ends

CHAPTER 2

MODERN DAY

They've got me on the 9th floor which is the homicide floor. It's nasty as ever and there are people everywhere. The floor is filthy, with rats running all over the place eating up guy's commissary in the middle of the night. They have toilets and showers in the middle of the cell, so there is no type of privacy whatsoever. I mean, this is the type of setting I've only seen on TV, but I guess this is the reality of it all. I can't believe that "me" of all people would end up in a place like this? What did I ever do to God for him to punish me like this?

Of all the things, maybe the real question should be, what did I do for God?

I made it to church often, and now that I think about it, I've been in church since I was a little boy, even paying my tithes. I was even the president of the Young People Willing Worker program. That should've counted for something in my book. I guess God don't show any favoritism huh?

"Aye, ole school, who is the people with the blue and orange jump suits on?" I asked my bunkie.

He was an older guy, maybe in his late forties. He looks like the type of guy who is no stranger to this environment. He has a baby fro with a few grey hairs in it and a beard to match, and he always keeps a toothpick in his mouth. He's a quiet guy, and barely has any words for anybody other than excuse me and thank you. Mainly all he does is read book after book.

"Those are inmates from the state penitentiary. They are either here to do two things. Fight their case or tell on somebody. Make sure you stay as far as possible away from them. They ain't nothing but bloodsuckers looking for trouble."

"What about the people who got their own TV's?"

"Oh, yeah, especially them. They are a part of what we call the H.R.Ds."

"…and what is that supposed to mean?" I asked with a puzzled look.

"H.R.Ds is the "Human Rats Department." They'll try and lure you in and figure out what type of information they can pull outta' you. If they get good leads, they run and tell the police and they get a time cut, and go home early.

"Dig that!" I looked at them with my nose turned up.

"Yeah, Young Blood. Where there is cheese there is a rat, and where there is a rat, there is a trap."

"What is that, some type of jail quote or something?"

"It's the truth, Young Blood. The best way to avoid the situation is to avoid the situation. So when you stay to yourself, you avoid all possible problems that may come your way. Don't be the cheese that they want to come and sniff out."

"That's why you stay to yourself?"

"That's how you do your time, Young Blood."

"Man, I ca---"

"Young blood," He cut me off while shaking his head, never ever complain about your current situation. It only makes it harder to do. You just gotta' do it! Remember this, struggle is ordained."

I nodded my head at what he was telling me and I soaked everything in like a human sponge. Like I said before, he looks like he's been down this road before, and if there is one thing I've learned growing up, that's always take in wisdom when it is being given.

"Oh, and by the way. I'm Cutty."

"Cutie?" I responded.

"No! Not Cutie. What, are you trying to say that I'm cute or something?" he joked.

"Naw, my bad, man."

"Cutty."

"Oh, I'm Bird."

We gave each other dap and I jumped back on top of my bunk.

I leaned over and looked down at him "Aye, Cutty?"

"What's up?"

"You've been down a long time, huh?"

"Bird, I've been locked up even before you were born."

"I'm eighteen."

"Exactly."

I laid back down on my rack staring at the ceiling tryna' block out all the noises that were going on around me. The bunks are connected to each other through the bars, there are no walls, and everyone can see and watch you all night if they wanted to. I swear, Detroit County jail has to be one of the worst jails ever created. Hell, this seems worse than the jails I've seen on CNN overseas. I guess like Cutty said, "it ain't nothin' to it, but to do it." I gotta' get down to the law library. I can't let them take me out like this.

"Chow time ladies. Let's go!" the guard yelled as they brought our food on the cart. The inmates prepare our food, and I have come to the realization that they aren't the best cooks around.

"What's for lunch, Cutty?"

"Bologna and cheese. You gonna' eat or are you still gonna' act like you can't eat jail food?"

I guess he noticed that I haven't eaten a single tray the last couple days I've been here. I just drink the juice and milk. I see people eat one minute, and puke it back up the next.

"Yeah, I guess I have to huh? I said before jumping down to grab my tray. Another day and another tray."

Inmates try to use the same methods of cooking drugs trying to apply that method to cooking food and it is not working out. Some inmates have become adjusted to the way life is in here and will actually enjoy it. Being away from a decent home-cooked meal for so long you will forget about it. Others gamble for inmates food just so they can get full. The way they feed you in here, you will die slowly.

Now I'm starting to see what Uncle Charlie was telling me when he said that life starts when the church ends. Let me continue telling the story.

CHAPTER 3

It's the first day of school, and I'm more than excited to start a new school year. I know middle school is going to be a blast and I can't wait. When I came up north, I was at the very end of elementary schooling. Gooney, Buck, Mike, Ike and I are all attending the same school. We all convinced our parents to let us go by ourselves since it not that far away and they bought it.

"Curtis!" my mom yelled.

"Yeah, mom."

"Let's go boy, your friends are here waiting on you."

I grabbed my backpack and ran to the front room where she was.

"Now, listen to me. Go to school and come straight home. Do you hear me?"

"Yes, mom, I hear you."

"Okay, now I made you a corned beef sandwich for lunch, so you shouldn't be hungry for the rest of the day," she handed me a brown paper bag.

"Moooom, stoooop" I complained because she licked her finger first before wiping my face.

"Shut up, boy!"

I opened the door and everyone was standing on the sidewalk waiting on me.

"Curtis, let's go, man," they all yelled.

"Okay, okay, okay, I'm coming."

It felt good to walk to school without your parents being there with you. It can be a bit embarrassing at times. It made us feel like we were on our own for a change. I guess that's what middle school was all about. On the brink of a new level, and we we're ready for it.

On the way to school, I observed some things that caught my attention. I don't know if I wasn't paying attention before in elementary school or if things are just that much different from the North and the South. The girls around here dressed different! They have their shirts tied around the back of them with their belly button piercings showing, and they have on the smallest shorts ever. I heard that they somehow came up with the name Daisy Dukes shorts and wearing lips full of shiny lip gloss.

I guess it's all a part of being in middle school. Most of the boys have either blue or red shirts on, and I can't seem to understand why someone would wear one solid color from head to toe, and not only that, but everyone pretty much has on the same thing. Must be a Detroit thing because down in Louisiana we wear whatever. It's like a big party up here. You have the seventh and eighth graders hanging out at their lockers laughing, joking, listening to their Sony Walkmans' and picking on all the new six graders walking by.

I saw one sixth grader's pants pulled so far up his back he couldn't walk in a straight line. He had to walk sideways up the hall like he had three legs. Imagine that! It was kind of funny though, but only till it happens to you of course. From what I've heard, the first week of school is called Freshman Week, where all the so-called upper classmen pick on all the six graders, giving them grief all week. I wasn't worried at all though because just about everyone from the neighborhood heard about me pulling out my knife this past summer.

So everybody pretty much assumed that I would do the same thing to them if they tried me. They were right because, since then, I have kept it on me at all times. I could tell that I wasn't like most kids my age because most of them enjoyed playing sports, watching videos on T.V. while on the other hand, I liked reading more than anything. Uncle Charlie told me once that there is a saying that says "If you want to hide something from a black man, put it in a book." Since he told me that, I have tried to read as much as I can, and in doing so, it helped with my vocabulary. I have always been interested in the universe and how it all came into existence.

Sometimes at night, I would look through my telescope into space at the cosmos. I tried to get my friends into it, but they really didn't care too much for it. To me, it was the most amazing thing to discover unknown faraway places. I always drifted into my own imagination of the outer limits of the earth. They say that "The Sky is the limit," but I believe that the limits of the sky are only in the eye of the beholder. Who knows, one day I may be an astronomer, and be the first black person to ever go into space and visit every planet. Most people called me weird because I was really concerned about learning.

I would always ask more questions than class time allowed. I was labeled a geek, although I'm far from looking like one. I would sit in the first row of science class and know every answer to every question that the teacher would ask. Sometimes the teacher would have me come up and teach the class things I knew about the stars. I didn't mind, because my mom always told me, "You will know when you are being yourself, and not like others because people will talk about you." That's when you know you're doing something right.

People still feared me because of that one little act of bravery that I pulled off last summer. I had a side of me that was a church boy, Preachers kid, and one of the Christian saints, but what others saw was a sixth grader with attitude. I didn't see the difference because to me, I was just being me. It was cool because I stayed loyal to my new family of friends.

"Curtis, what's up?" Gooney said while approaching me in the hallway after I came out my class.

"What's up, Gooney?"

"Middle school is a whole lot more fun than elementary huh?"

"Yea, and I can't believe how much different it is compared to back home in Louisiana."

"Yeah, I know right!"

"What's up, y'all?" Mike and Ike walked up from behind.

"What's up, where y'all headed?"

"It's lunch time, let's go."

"Aye, anybody seen Buck?" Gooney wondered.

"He's probably already in there."

　　　　We put our bags in the locker and grabbed our lunches and headed to the lunchroom, and what do you know, Buck was already sitting down waiting on us. I went and met him at the table while the others went to get their lunch trays.

"What's up, Buck?"

"What's up, Curtis? Middle school is fun huh?"

"You already know, man, I have a little situation already."

"Buck, it's the first day of school."

"Yeah, man, some kid tried to jump me in the restroom because I was a sixth grader, and not to mention I'm white with cornrows in my hair. They started saying that I was a "Wigger.""

"What does that mean?" I was confused about the northern slang...

"It's a white person trying to be black."

"Oh, who though?"

"Alright, don't look, but they're sitting right behind us."

I turned around.

"I said, don't look, Curtis!" he shouted.

"Are they eighth graders? They are huge."

"Yea, man, and I think I will have to deal with them after school."

"Why do you think that?"

"Because they said it wasn't over."

I turned back around and it was four of them looking our way. One of them balled up his fist and started pounding it into his other hand like he meant business. I guess now that he sees that I'm with Buck I'm in for a real treat after school as well. I wasn't worried about it at all because I knew that I had my blade on my hip, and I was eager to use it if I needed to. The rest of the gang came to the table we were, and I could tell that they knew that something was wrong. They saw me and Buck looking back and forth over at the eighth graders.

"What's up, y'all? Gooney said while sitting down with her tray.

"Buck has a problem."

"Already? With whom?" Mike asked.

"Don't look, but they are right behind us."

They all turned around.

"Don't look, y'all!" I shouted.

"So what we gonna' do?" asked Ike.

"We gonna' do what we supposed to do and that is stick together," I gestured.

We all sat there eating our food while keeping a close eye on them as well. We had to walk past them to leave the lunchroom, and we tried our hardest to wait them out, but they stayed seated until we made our move. It was only one way in, and one way out.

We stood up and they immediately gave us eye contact. The closer we got to them, the more my gut was telling me that they were going to try something. I lead the way while everyone else stayed close behind me. I made sure that Gooney was close by just in case they tried something slick. We all walked past except for Buck. Don't know why he was walking so slowly, but I do remember him telling us to save some milk in the cartons and give them to him and before we knew it, Buck had emptied the whole tray on their laps, and ran over to where we were and we all burst out laughing.

"After school sixth grader," the oversized kid yelled in anger with a lap full of milk.

We all left out the lunchroom still laughing at the stunt Buck just pulled and headed to our lockers.

"Aye, y'all, meet up right here when school is over? We gonna' go out together." I suggested, and everyone agreed.

It's 2:58 in the afternoon and school is just about over. I can barely pay attention to what the teacher is saying because I'm too busy thinking about what's going to happen after school. Although I knew I had my knife with me and wouldn't mind using it, the thought of doing just that haunted me ever since lunch was over. Maybe this is when someone will call my bluff, and realize that I'm too scared to do so. Or maybe I will get too nervous and end up dropping it, and one of them uses it on me.

It's 2:59pm and my body is beginning to perspire. I even have sweat in the palm of my hands. In one minute the bell will ring, and then it's going to be a helluva' journey on my way back home.

I start putting everything away as the time ticks away.

Tick….tock…tick…tock...I can hear every second on the clock as if I had a stethoscope in my ears. The teacher is uttering words that I can't even understand and can no longer hear.

"Okay class, school is over. Make sure you have everything on the syllabus by next week."

I heard the bell ring, but I couldn't move. It felt like I was stuck in my seat. At first it seemed like the bell was taking forever to sound and now it seems like it was happening too fast. My palms are sweaty and I keep opening and closing them looking at the clock and hoping that time would rewind back to 2:59pm.

"Mr. Books," the teacher came to my desk.

"Uh, huh?"

"Class is over, honey. You can go home now."

"Oh uh…okay."

I grabbed my things before I left the classroom and I peeked my head out before entering the hallway.

"Mr. Books?"

"Yes, Ms. Green Waters?"

"Who are you looking for?"

"Umm….nobody, Ms. Green Waters. I'm leaving now."

I walked out and headed to my locker, and everyone was there waiting on me.

"Man, what took you so long, Curtis?" Buck asked.

"I had to talk to my teacher about school work," I lied.

"She gave you school homework already?"

"Yup!" I looked around.

"Let's go!" Gooney suggested.

Every step we took towards the door we were looking from left to right making sure that none of the eighth graders jumped out of nowhere. Once we got outside there were people everywhere. Some getting picked up by their parents, some waiting on the department of transportation, and some getting on the yellow school bus. We started walking home, and by the time we walked halfway down the street, we had company waiting for us.

"Hey, sixth graders?" It was our after school fate waiting on us.

We stopped dead in our tracks as they started walking towards us.

"What we gonna' do, Curtis?" Ike asked in panic mode.

"Like I said earlier, we gonna' stick together."

"Buck, wait!" Gooney shouted.

Buck started walking towards them, and I already knew what was coming up next. Buck didn't even care if it was twenty to one fight just as long as he swung first.

I remember one time over the summer, he fought a 12th grader, and got whooped, but he stood his ground.

I walked behind him waiting on him to make the first move.

"PLOW!" Buck punched one of them in the face, and that's when the brawl started.

Even Gooney jumped into the action and blow after blow we were keeping each others back.

"Hold up, hold up, wait!" one of them yelled as I instantly pulled out my blade.

They backed up and it was blood all over my clothes. I had mistakenly stabbed one of them in the arm, and one of the others nose was bleeding.

"I got stabbed, man," he yelled while the others moved out of the way hoping they weren't next.

"Stop right there!" someone yelled from behind us, and when we all turned around it was the security guard. My shirt was off, and I had the blade in my hand. I couldn't toss it because his eyes were locked on me.

"Give me the knife, son," he ordered.

"I found it on the ground," I quickly tried to justify the situation.

He walked up to me and took it, putting it in his van. Moments later the police came, and took everyone to the precinct jail, and sat us all in the waiting room.

"Curtis, what we gonna' do now?" Gooney was scared.

"I don't know, but I hope they don't put us in a cell."

Buck was looking at his fist because they were swollen, and the eighth graders had the look of disgust on their faces because they had been defeated. The guard told us that they had called our parents to come and pick us up. They tried to get the one I stabbed to press charges on me, but he refused. He said that he fell on some glass that was on the ground. The cut was just a scrape anyway, so they didn't press the issue.

They tried to charge me with assault and battery. I told them that I found the knife on the ground and that I picked it up so nobody would get hurt. They bought my story and left it alone. One the other hand, I'm gonna' have to explain this to my mom because I know she will be here any minute now. I know for sure that my punishment will consist of me not going outside for a while.

"Yeah, whatever, cop. Meet me in my cell and let's see how much you gonna' talk like that. I got them hands, boy, for real. I'm 7 mile all day, family." Someone yelled to the police that had him cuffed behind.

"Who is that?" Gooney asked.

"He's this kid named Tom Tom. He's from 7 mile. His dad went to jail for killing his brother over some money from a one- on- one basketball game. His mother sent him to his father because she couldn't raise him. He was getting to big and out of control," Said Buck.

"He looks crazy," Gooney stared at him as he bounced through the hallway taunting the police officers.

"Man, thanks for having my back y'all," said Buck.

"What, you thought we wasn't?" I asked.

"I never had anyone back me up the way y'all did."

"Well, now you know, man. We are friends, and that's what friends do," said Ike.

We all sat there in silence reflecting on the day's events.

Gooney broke the silence "just one more thing, Curtis, How did your shirt come off?" she started laughing.

"I have no idea."

"I looked up and saw a bird. I'm like, are we fighting pigeons or what?"

"From now on man, we gonna' call you 'Bird'," Mike chimed in through hard laughter.

"Yea, okay, y'all got down," I joined in on their joke.

"CURTIS MARCEL BOOKS!" I heard my name being yelled through the building and I knew exactly who it was.

"BOY, YOU BETTER BRING YO TAIL HERE NOW! WHAT THE HELL DID YOU DO?"

"Nothing ma, I ….."

"WAM!" she slapped me across the right side of my face in front of everyone.

"Argghh ma…..argghh" I ached in pain.

"Just wait till we get home. I'm gonna' tear you a new butt hole. Just wait!"

I didn't even bother looking up. I just kept my head low as we walked out the prescient. She was still yelling in my ear from the jail to the car, to all the way home.

"You think you in some trouble, now. I'm gonna' show you trouble, and I'm a spell it out on your behind just so you know exactly what I mean."

WAM! She smacked me again…

CHAPTER 4

CHURCH

"God is good."

"All the time."

"And all the time."

"God is good."

"I want to talk to you all today about trials. Yes! I know we all have them, and what's even more important to remember is that we all have to go through them. Many of us try to run from them, and I can't understand why. Maybe it's because we are not deeply rooted in our word. (The congregation became quiet). The bible tells us that God has not given us the spirit of fear, but of POWER. (He shouted) So, if you will, beloved, please turn your bibles to Genesis chapter three. I know we are familiar with this passage, but are we REALLY familiar with it? If you closely look at the title of this chapter it is titled, "The Fall of Man." What man? Who are you talking about, Pastor? You may ask. Not Adam, although we are about to read about Adam, but I want you to understand that if we are reading this book called the Bible, and we cannot see ourselves in it, then what's the point of reading it? Surely, it's not just for bedtime stories, at least I hope it's not. What are we gaining when we read? How are we interpreting the words? And how does this apply to our lives?

May we all stand for the reading of His Word. Starting at verse one.

(New International Version) Verse 1: Now the serpent was more crafty than any of the wild animals the Lord God had made. He said to the woman, "Did God really say, You must not eat from any tree in the garden?"

Verse 2: The woman said to the serpent, "We may eat fruit from the trees in the garden.

Verse 3: But God did say, You must not eat fruit from the tree that is in the middle of the garden, and you must not touch it, or you will die."

Verse 4: "You will not surely die," the serpent said to the woman.

Verse 5: For God knows that when you eat of it your eyes will be opened, and you will be like God, knowing good and evil."

Verse 6: When the woman saw that the fruit of the tree was good for food and pleasing to the eye, and also desirable for gaining wisdom, she took some and ate it. She also gave some to her husband, who was with her, and he ate it.

Verse 7: Then the eyes of both of them were opened, and they realized they were naked; so they sewed fig leaves together and made coverings for themselves.

We go through life running from issues that we have the God given power to create and get rid of everyday. Every day we are faced with trials to propel us through life. There is not a day that I don't have a trial, and I'm your pastor, but I don't run from it. I face them head on. I heard someone say one time that, "If you kill the head, the body will follow." So when faced with adversity think about it, analyze it, look at all dimensions of it and find your way through. Through every tunnel that may seem like it's dark, know that there is light at the end of that tunnel. When you start looking for external forces to come and guide you through it, you've already lost the battle. Be confident, know your self-worth, welcome new challenges and trials because when they come to you, you will gain from them. Once you start running from what God has ordained, you add fuel to the fire and make it worse. We complain about jobs, we complain about money, we complain about not being given the opportunities that others have, but we are not thankful for the life that we already have. If we just hold out, look at your neighbor, and say "if you just hold out…"

The congregation repeated…

"God will make a way."

The congregation repeated…

I'm sitting in my regular seat in the choir stand behind the pulpit. My grandfather just got up to give his sermon. My butt is still sore from my mom whooping me like crazy last week. I would have rather gone on punishment for a month. She almost did that too. After I finally caught my breath, I was able to explain to her that I was just trying to protect myself. At the end of the day, she still let me have it. Of course, she gave me this drawn out speech on how I'm supposed to go about certain situations, and how I can avoid them. It seems to me that even though they tell you how to avoid things, it doesn't stop those things from coming around you.

In church, you see people getting excited, dancing all over the place, and speaking in crazy languages that nobody understands. When I look out the window, I see females doing the exact same thing. They are dancing to whatever is coming from the trunks of cars parked outside, trying to keep up with the fast lyrics. I mean, what's the difference? The people I see outside the window are just as happy as the people in the church and it baffles me because I don't understand what my grandmother is trying to keep me from. They say it's two different worlds, but is it? And if it is, which world am I really part of? My mom will be at the club all night on Saturday, and then in church singing hymns to the almighty God on Sunday. We are struggling to make ends meet and my cousin Tim always have a lot of money and he don't even have a job. Uncle Charlie never comes to church but he's always taking his communion at home. Seems like he's doing pretty good to me.My grandfather talking about Jesus turning water into wine, and outside it's a line wrapped around the corner at the beer and wine store.

I wonder if there is really such a thing as this Heaven or Hell? I once read that the diameter of the earth is approximately seven thousand nine hundred and twenty six miles. If they know the diameter of the earth, how can there be a Hell under it?

"Life starts when the church ends" is what Uncle Charlie said to me, and I'm still yet to crack the atom on that. I heard my grandmother tell the girls here at church that they shouldn't wear skirts that are too short, and that the skirt should come down to their ankles. I like the girls with the short skirts, and I know for a fact that they feel a lot more comfortable when it's scorching hot outside. I guess I've always been a person who thinks outside the box, while others are like the hamster on the wheel, thinking they are actually going somewhere but all along are stagnant. They say, "Train up a child in the way he should go and when he gets old he won't depart from it." Hell, I think the church is teaching me how to be more of a square than anything.

My mom didn't make it to church today, so I went with my grandma. I'm so glad that they didn't cook today, so I know I'm going straight home.

"Grand boy, you ready?"

"Grandma, I was ready before I left home."

"Boy," she gave me the look.

"Sorry."

On my way home I, couldn't wait to get around with my friends. Driving down the street I see Uncle Charlie sitting on his porch. My mom was coming out of his house with a bag of sugar in her hand. When we pulled to the curb, she was meeting us at the car door.

"Hi, Mom," I said while getting out the car, giving her a hug.

"Hey baby, how was church?"

"Girl, we had a beautiful time," my grandma chimed into the conversation. "What you doing over there?"

"I had to borrow some sugar from Charlie so I can make some yams."

"You cooked, Ma?" I said excitedly, because she doesn't cook big meals often. Usually she would just open up a can of glory greens, fry some chicken, and call it a day. Sometimes at night, she would make some breakfast. No matter what time it was, breakfast was always the number one option to cook.

"Yes, I did. So, go in there and clean up your room."

"K," I said running in the house.

I grabbed all the clothes that were on the floor and threw them under the bed so I could hurry up and run back outside to meet up with my crew.

"Finished," I yelled as I blew by my mom, who was still in the kitchen cooking.

"Young Buck," Uncle Charlie yelled as I stepped outside. "Come here real quick. Lemme' holla at you."

I ran over to him and sat down next to him on the porch.

"What's up, young Buck?"

"Nothing."

He was drinking out of a little glass that was not even half full with water and a couple ice cubes. I didn't know that water came in so many different labels and bottles. The one he held had the words "Gin" on it. My mom always has one that says "Vodka," and she never gives me any. She always tells me that tap water makes you think better, so I should drink it more often.

"Young Buck, I need you to do something for me."

"What's that?"

"I need you to take this paper bag over to 11th street for me. It's the only house that has two dog houses in the front yard. When you get there tell them that Uncle Charlie sent you. You gonna' give them the paper bag and they're gonna' give you a duffle bag in return to give back to me."

"Alright cool, but can I have some of that water you drinking?" I asked with a smile on my face, hoping that he would give me some of this exclusive water that only grown-ups seem to be drinking.

"Nawl, young Buck, you can't have this over here."

"Why not?" I said waiting on him to give me a good answer.

"You'll understand later, okay?"

"Uncle Charlie, it's only water."

"Young Buck, just take this package over on 11th street for me, okay?" He handed me the paper bag.

I took it and walked off the porch.

"Young Buck," he yelled.

"What's up?"

"You know life starts when the church ends right?"

I looked and him, hunched my shoulders, and went to take the paper bag over on 11th street.

I don't have my blade anymore because the police took it the day we had gotten into that situation at school. I sure hope I don't run into those bullies again. I folded up the paper bag and tucked it into my tighty-whities just in case some of the kids thought I had candy. I don't know what's in the bag to begin with, but I know for sure that Uncle Charlie probably ain't selling no candy.

I got to 11th street and immediately saw the house that Uncle Charlie told me to go to. Just as he said, there were two doghouses in the front yard. There wasn't even any grass, just all dirt. It's broad daylight, but as I got closer I could hear music coming from the inside, like they were throwing a party. I walked through the gate, and all of a sudden, "woof, woof, woof,woof!" Two Doberman Pinschers came out of nowhere, barking and foaming at the mouth. I jumped back so fast that I tripped and fell on my back. I thought I was about to be devoured, but they were chained up to a tire that didn't reach that far from the doghouses.

"Who dat?"

I looked up and saw someone yelling from the inside. I got up, brushed my clothes off, and stood there. "It's Bird. I have something for you from Uncle Charlie."

"Oh, come on in, Cuz," he gestured.

I walked up to the door, which was already cracked open, looked behind me at the other house next door and down the street in paranoia. I'm a little scared because this is reminding me of some of those movies I seen on TV. I pushed the door slowly, and it made a squeaky noise. I looked in and saw no furniture, only crates in the front room. A picture of a blonde hair blue-eyed man was on the wall similar to the one we have at church and in most of the houses I've seen before. Everyone seems to have this picture.

"I'm in here," someone yelled from the back.

I walked in and looked to the right. There was a big fat black guy in the kitchen at the stove cooking. I wondered how he was cooking food and there was no furniture to even sit at, only a glass table in the dining area.

"What's up, Cuz? You got something for me?"

"Uh…yeah. Uncle Charlie sent me around here to give you something."

"Oh yeah! Well, where it is?"

"Oh uh… hold on." I reached down in my drawls and pulled out the brown paper bag. "Here it is." I handed him the bag.

"Uncle Charlie told you to put that there?"

"Oh naw, I just figured that it was the best thing to do."

"Is that right?" he said as if he was surprised. "Not too bad for a youngsta'." He looked in the bag. I was trying to look myself because I was curious as to what was in it. He looked at me when he saw I was trying to be nosey. "Watchu' say your name was?"

"Bird."

"Oh snap!" he yelled then ran back to the stove. He started stirring whatever he had in the pot. Whatever it was must have been boiling hot because steam was coming from it like it was fire in it. Moments later he headed to the back. I'm looking around the room trying to figure out why there is no furniture around. The only table that was in there had a big box of baking soda on it. He must wash his clothes often, or clean his shoes daily.

"Bird."

I turned around and he threw a black backpack at me, just like Uncle Charlie said he would. I put it on my back like he told me to and proceeded to the door. "I see you keep the baking soda to keep your shoes clean and white"

He looked down with a puzzled look on his face rubbing his long beard and laughed, "you silly, youngsta."

"Aye, Bird." He called me as I reached the door

"What's up?"

"I'll see you soon, all right?"

I just hunched my shoulders and walked out.

"Woof, woof, woof, woof!" The dogs jumped out of nowhere again. I had forgotten about them. My heart almost jumped out of my chest. I walked past them and headed back to Uncle Charlie's house.

When I got back, there he was sitting on the porch smoking a cigarette.

"Young Buck, you made it back huh?"

"Yeah, it was no big deal." I took off the bag and handed it to him. He opened it up and looked inside. I tried to be nosey again to see what I was carrying.

"What is it?" I asked.

"Young Buck, I'm gonna' tell you like this. It ain't no school books, that's for sure." He stood up and went into the house. Shortly after, he came back out. "You know, I really appreciate what you just did for me."

"Anytime."

He smiled, pulled out a pocket full of money, and gave me a twenty-dollar bill.

"Now listen Young Buck, if you do this for me every Sunday I'll give you twenty dollars every time. If you do it on the regular, I'll give you more."

"Really? And all I gotta' do is just take a brown bag and bring a duffle bag back?" I asked eagerly.

"That's right!"

"Cool," I held the twenty in the sunlight. I heard that's how you can tell if it's real or not. I don't really know what to look for, but I see my mom do it all the time. I walked off the porch and went home.

"Hey, Bird, what's up?"

"What's up, Gooney?" I walked over to her house.

"Where you coming from?"

"I was over at Uncle Charlie's house. He just gave me twenty dollars. Let's go to the store and get some candy."

"Okay, let me put on my shoes." She got up and ran in the house while I sat there with the twenty in the sun, still looking through it.

"Let's go!" She came running back.

"We about to get a whole lot of candy for twenty dollars, huh?"

"Yeah we are, but what did Uncle Charlie give you money for?"

"He wanted me to do something for him."

"Like what?" she wondered.

"Gooney, why are you asking so many questions?"

"I just wanted to know because he wanted to give me money before too."

"For what?"

"I don't know, I didn't ask."

We approached the store and there was a group of boys standing in front. They all had on blue. A few of them had on a blue scarf around their head, like the ones my mom wears at night before she goes to sleep. Some of them had the scarf hanging out of their back pocket. We got closer to the door and they looked at us. We acted like we didn't even see them and walked in.

"Gooney, get whatever you want," I said as I walked straight to the candy sections to get some Boston Baked Beans and some Lemon Heads. It's like candy heaven, and with twenty dollars, I knew I was going to be eating candy for the rest of the month.

"Can I get some of these?"

"Gooney, I said get whatever you want. I'll be waiting at the counter when you're done." I stood at the register waiting on Gooney to hurry up. Every time I looked at the door I could see one of the guys outside looking through the window.

"Gooney, hurry up!" I yelled.

"I'm coming, I'm coming." She said with a hand full of licorice and some Now and Laters as she ran up the aisle. "What you looking like that for? You said get whatever I wanted."

"Girl, I ain't trippin'." I paid the cashier the money for our candy and he put it in two separate bags. I gave Gooney her bag and we started walking towards the door. I could still see one of the guys peeking through the window. When he saw me and Gooney on our way, he hurried up and vanished. I knew it was going to be an issue, but I still had to go out. I couldn't act scared in front of a girl, let alone Gooney.

We walked outside and everybody was looking at us. It was about six of them, and they all had on royal blue. The first thing that came to my mind was that this must be one of those dance groups that's trying to get on Apollo or something. I could tell that Gooney knew something was wrong by the way she was lagging behind.

"Aye, what you got in that bag homie?" One of them yelled with a deep voice.

"Some candy, why?"

"Because I want it, that's why." He started walking up on me and his crew followed. They surrounded me in a circle and I looked them in the eyes, holding my ground the best way I could with my bag in both hands.

"You can't have this," I told him.

"Oh yeah, and what makes you think that?"

I reached for my knife, but forgot that I didn't have it anymore. I looked at Gooney, then back at him.

"Whop!" I swung first and hit him in the jaw. "Run Gooney!" I yelled and she took off running as they immediately started jumping me. They were kicking me so hard in the stomach that it felt like my ribs were about to break. I just curled up in a ball and kept taking the beating.

Moments later, the kicking had stopped, and when I had opened my eyes they were all gone. Not only did they whoop me badly, they didn't leave a single piece of candy behind. I got up and started walking home, holding my stomach. Every time I breathed my stomach would ache with a sharp pain. I looked up and Gooney was running towards me with Buck, Mike, and Ike.

"Bird, you okay?"

"I'll be alright. Arrgghhh! Don't touch me there!"

"Sorry."

"Just help me to the porch."

We walked to the porch and she already had some ice in a Bucket.

"You already knew I was gonna' get whooped, huh?"

"Well, when you punched him in the face that hard, I knew they were gonna' try and beat you badly."

"Yeah, and they took all my candy too."

"Well, not all of it." She held the bag she had in the air.

"Who was it?" Buck asked.

"Some boys in blue. They all had on blue from head to toe."

"They were Crips."

"Some who?"

"Crips, it's a gang."

"Ya'll talking about gangs, like what we see on TV?"

"Yep."

"Man, I didn't even know Detroit had gangs."

"Yeah man, L.A, Chicago and New York ain't the only ones."

"Arrgghh. My ribs hurt but that's okay. I'll get them back, just watch."

Life Starts When The Church Ends

CHAPTER 5

"Boy, come here," my mom yelled as I tried to sneak past her.

"Huh?"

"Huh my butt. What happened to your face?" She grabbed me by my jaw and turned my head to the side to see my instant black eye.

"I got into a fight."

"A fight? With who?"

"Some boys at the store."

"The store? What the hell were you doing at the store?" She said as she stepped back folding her arms waiting to hear why I went to the store without her permission.

I couldn't tell her that Uncle Charlie gave me some money because then she would ask more questions than I wanted to answer.

"Boy, I'm talkin' to you. Why did you go to the store without my permission?"

"I don't know. I'm sorry. I found a dollar bill on the sidewalk and walked to the store. I didn't go by myself, Gooney went with me."

"Oh, so you think you grown now huh? You think you can just up and go to the store whenever you feel like it huh?"

I really didn't know how to explain myself so I just remained quiet. I felt like I was almost in the clear of not telling her everything that happened just moments ago.

"Who is it?" my mom yelled at whoever was knocking on the door.

"Gooney. Is Bir—I mean Curtis coming outside?"

"Come in here, girl." my mom ordered.

Gooney came in looking puzzled. I looked her in the eyes and shook my head. She put her attention back on my mom.

"Hi, Ms. Lilyan."

"Sit down, Gooney."

Gooney took a seat across from where my mom and I were.

"Were you at the store when Curtis got into a fight?"

"Uh…"

"Don't 'uh' me, girl. Were you or were you not?"

I could tell that Gooney really didn't want to say the wrong thing that could get me in more trouble than I was already in. She didn't want my mom to tell her mom about us sneaking off to the store. Gooney kept looking back and forth between my mom and me.

"Yes."

"Well, what happened?"

"One of the guys was trying to mess with him, and he told me to run home."

"Is that right?" She said while looking at me. I just hunched my shoulders. "Ya'll a mess, you know that?"

I just smiled because I knew that those were words that I was in the clear. My mom just shook her head.

"Can I go back outside, Momma?"

"I guess boy, go ahead."

"I'll be back, Gooney. Let me change my shirt." I ran to the back while Gooney stayed in the front room.

"Gooney, what you doing over there at Charlie's?" my mom started questioning Gooney

"My mom sent me over there to get some sugar."

"Some sugar huh?"

"Yeah."

"Okay, now Gooney, you better watch out. I see you are developing real quick. You better be careful in these streets, and don't grow up too fast. You hear me?"

"Okay, Ms. Lilyan. I will."

"Tell your mom I said 'hello'."

"Ready?" I came running from the back. Gooney stood up and we headed back outside.

"What was that about?" Gooney asked me.

"I tried to sneak past her but she saw me coming in."

"Who is that?" Gooney said referring to a burgundy and gold Ford Excursion coming down the street, with the music sounding like Godzilla coming down the block.

"I don't know, but look at those rims."

As the truck was coming down the street, it slowed up a bit as it got close to my house. It pulled into the driveway and I could feel the vibrations from the speakers beating through my chest. The music stopped and the driver door opened. It was my cousin Tim.

"That's my cousin, Tim. What's up, Tim?"

"What up, Lil' Curt? What's good, Cuz?"

"When did you get that?"

"I just picked it up a few hours ago." I couldn't help but stare at my cousin's jewelry and Cartier glasses with the diamond specs.

"Boy, what is that?" my mom said coming outside looking at Tim and his monster truck.

"What up, cuz?" I just picked this bad boy up a few hours ago."

"Now you ain't gotta' worry about it smoking all the time huh?" I chimed in and my mom and Tim busted out laughing.

"Bird," I hear someone whispering my name. When I turned about it was Buck. My mom and

 Tim went in the house and I walked over to see what Buck wanted.

"What's up, Buck?"

"I just saw those Crips that jumped you."

"Really? Where at?"

"At the park down the street."

"What you wanna' do?"

"I say we all get together and go down there."

"I'll be right back," Said Gooney.

"Naw' Gooney, you stay here," I suggested.

"Naw', I'm coming! I ain't scared! I ain't scared!" she repeated with a high pitched voice showing her arms.

"Okay, well let's go. Where's Mike and Ike?" I said looking down the street. I saw them sitting on the porch playing Connect Four. "Let me run and tell my mom that I'm going to the park."

"Man, she ain't gonna' know you gone. Your cousin just came over. They probably ain't even thinking about you." Buck added, making a point.

I thought about it for a second, and we all headed to the park down the street. Even though we were outnumbered, and had a girl with us, it didn't matter. We've been riding with each other for a quite some time and had created a family-like bond.

They seemed to think that I'm some type of silent bad boy ever since I pulled out that knife on a couple of occasions. To them I am hard, but to me, I'm just tryna' maintain the image that they painted on me. I felt tough when I was around them, and it seemed like every time I was put in a position of fear I showed something completely different, to stay cool. Then again, I could just be a church boy who's not quite what my family wants me to be.

We could see the Crips sitting on the jungle gym, eating my candy. That made me even more mad. We really didn't have a plan, and I didn't know how we were going to conquer them since we were outnumbered. I guess we'll just be making a statement.

"What we gon' do, Bird?" Gooney asked.

"Just follow me," I replied.

We started walking and by the time we got close to them they noticed us. I picked up a stick that I saw along the way and they all stood up.

"What's up, fool? You want some more?" One of the older ones said.

We didn't say a word. We just stood there waiting on somebody to make the first move. My crew was waiting on me to strike first and vice versa. I'm waiting on one of them to strike first because me doing it is out of the question.

"What you gonna' do, boy?" They taunted me again, while they were eating my candy.

I looked over at Buck and he had his fist balled up. I knew he was ready for action because his face was red and he was biting down on his bottom lip. He must get that from the white side of his family.

"Buck, wait!" Gooney yelled as Buck took off running toward them, yelling like a mad man. I took off right behind him with the stick in my hand. There were about eight of them, but after Buck took the initiative to strike first, three of the younger ones took off running in the opposite direction. One of them fell, and I ran straight to him first. With the stick in my hand I struck him across his legs as hard as I could. "WAM!" He yelled out loud as he immediately grabbed his knee caps. I struck him again and hit the back of his hands. "PLOP!" I tried to break every bone, but ended up breaking the stick instead.

I looked around and saw Buck on top of somebody beating them in the face. Gooney was putting in work on someone while Mike was holding him around the neck.

"Okay, okay, okay!" one of them yelled in submission.

Buck was still putting in work until I ran over and pulled him off. Stuck in a trance, He was looking around like he lost something.

"Buck!" I shook him. "Snap out of it!"

"Oh, my bad, man. Let's go!"

I ran and grabbed the left over candy.

We took off running down the street, laughing as our hearts were still beating fast.

"Man, did you see that?" I asked as we chuckled about the fight we'd just had.

"Did you see Gooney giving him a noogie?" Mike stated.

We bursted out laughing again, eating the remains of my left over candy while sitting on Gooney's porch.

I have a real genuine love for my friends, and I know that they have love for me. We have a natural bond and would have each other's back no matter what. It's like we are the typical black family in the projects but different mothers while poppa' is out being a rolling stone.While sitting on the porch, I realized that this is a bond that I want for life. The bond of a lifetime was right here on this porch, and I wouldn't trade it for the world.

Life Starts When The Church Ends

CHAPTER 6

MODERN DAY

Heading back to my cell from a court hearing on my case and they are trying to get me to take a plea bargain for nine years. They must be out they damn minds if they think I'm gonna' take a plea for something I know I didn't do. My mom told me that she was going to get me a paid lawyer because this court appointed lawyer I have is acting like he is working against me. They all want to see me go down. I guess that's how the system works. My grandfather told me before he died that once you're in the system it's hard to get out. I'm sure he wasn't prophesying my future, because he told me that at a young age.

My mom and cousin Tim were in the audience in the courtroom. I could barely look my mom in the face because she looked like she was about to burst into tears at any second. It was good to have her there for support though, because I needed all the support I could get. I could get a natural life sentence if this case goes to trial and I'm not trying to take a chance and let this system railroad me to the moon.

I just got back to my spot and everyone was layin' on their racks, chillin'. My bunkie went to health care or to the law library. I've been down in court all day, and haven't had anything to eat. I grabbed my box of commissary from under the bunk and noticed that someone has been in it. If it's one thing I learned in jail, it's don't mess with someone's zoom-zooms and wham-whams.

I immediately started looking around my bunkie's area, trying to see if there were some empty candy wrappers lying around. To my surprise, there wasn't. I started looking around the cell, and these fools in here acting like they don't know what went down since I've been gone.

I started giggling. "Oh, so ya'll actin' like everything is everything, huh?"

"What!" one of my cellmates jumped to his defense.

"You heard me. Someone has been in my commissary."

"Well, it wasn't me."

"Well, I can't tell. You the first one to snatch it out the air."

"If it don't apply, let it fly," another cellmate mumbled from across the room, then started laughing.

"Oh, so you think it's funny?" I responded heated and ready to fight.

 The guy I was talking to at first pointed to him as if he was the one who stole from me. When I looked over at him, he was chewing. I immediately went over to his bunk and stood over him. I said, "You know exactly what it is, homie."

"Oo..don't—"

I pulled him off his bunk down to the ground and started choking him. He was trying to loosen my grip from around his neck because his face was turning Easter pink. The inmates from other cells were roaring and yelling "fight, fight, fight!" I'm beating him in the face with my right hand, while still holding him around the neck with my left. I got rushed from behind by one of his homeboys, and they both started stomping me in the back. This white boy's face was as pink as a bottle of Pepto Bismol, with a look on his face like he wanted to kill me. I curled up so they couldn't get me in the face, and moments later they must've gotten tired because they suddenly stopped.

"Stupid NIGGER!" one yelled after he spat on me.

They must not know about the forty-eight laws of power. "Crush your enemy totally and never let him recover."

They went back to their side of the cell and I went to my bunk. I laid down on my side, with my back towards them. I cut a small strip of my sheet off, about as long as a shoestring, and wrapped it around my hands. I sat there for a minute or two, and waited for the right opportunity. About five minutes passed, and one of them went to take a leak. I followed right behind him, bingo!

As soon as he started pissing, I took the string and walked up right behind him, unnoticed, put the string around his neck and pulled back. He started coughing and gasping for air, and pissing all over the place as I dragged him down to the ground. The inmates were roaring again, and then his boy noticed. I didn't care because my only concern was trying to kill this white boy. Not literally, but just send him a message.

"Arrgghh!" His boy gave me a blow to the rib cage, right under my left arm, causing me to lose my wind. By that time, the one I was choking wasn't even putting up a fight. When I looked at him, he had turned blue and passed out. I started tussling with the other one.

As he threw a few punches and connected, I started countering his moves. I knew which punch he was about to throw next. He was about to swing an overhand right, and follow up with a left hook.

Just like clockwork the punches came, and just as he was throwing them I knocked his arms outta' the way. It knocked him off balance, and I had a perfect angle behind the ear. "WHAM!" Once I hit him, he fell over into the shower and went to sleep. I walked over and stood over him as the guards came rushing in. They put me in cuffs and proceeded to take me to the hole.

Walking alongside the gate, I kept looking at the boy I choked out and just before he was outta' sight he started moving. "Thank you, Jesus, I didn't kill him." That would be been another problem that I would have had to deal with.

Now, I'm in the hole and one thing comes to mind. Uncle Charlie told me that, "life starts when the church ends." I'm beginning to get a more in depth understanding of that. The reality is starting to set in. Where is God now?

CHAPTER 7

CHURCH

"Go on, go up there."

"I don't want to go…Why I gotta' go?"

"Boy, you need some prayer. So, get up and go to the altar."

I hate it when my auntie makes me go up to the altar for prayer. Everybody in the church stares at you all crazy, like they can't wait to see you hollering and jumping around like you're a clown or something. It seems like the preacher tries to push you down as soon as he places his hands on your forehead.

I got up and slowly walked towards the front. I was taking my time, hoping that he would be finished before I could get up to there. There were so many people waiting to hear a word from the Lord. I didn't think I needed a word from God, because if he wanted to say something to me he would appear in a burning bush or something. Hell, He did it for Moses, why couldn't he do it for me? That cracks me up every time I think about it.

There is one thing I don't understand though. If the Bible talks about a snake talking, God speaking to Moses through a burning bush, and Moses' rod turning into a snake, why aren't these stunts happening today? I mean, I see it on TV, but what about it happening in reality? I guess the Bible is something like a bedtime story. That explains why I have dreams about a red devil with a pitchfork and red tail trying to get me to come to Hell with him. Where does it say that the devil is a red man with horns in his head anyway?

I was halfway down the aisle and there was one person left waiting to get prayed for. If I could just stall out for a few minutes, I would be free from the big man with the hands the size of Shaq trying to push me down. I looked up at my grandmother and her eyes were closed. She must've felt me looking at her because her eyes opened immediately. She smiled, went over to the preacher, and whispered something in his ear.

I know she didn't just tell him what I think she did. She sure did. "Well, I'll be," I said to myself.

"Come up here, son," the preacher motioned for me to come directly to him. I'm looking at who was next, wondering if they were going to protest or something because I was cutting in front of their blessing. That's how I looked at it, but she just smiled and moved to the side. I walked up, and he had a big bottle of olive oil in one hand, pouring some in the palm of the other.

"How are you doing, son?"

I nodded my head, "I'm good."

"What do you want the Lord to do for you today?"

I just hunched my shoulders as if he was supposed to tell me. He's the type of preacher with the smooth words and hands that could knock King Kong down. My grandmother will often invite him to come and speak at the church when she felt like the members were backsliding too far. I know for a fact that the olive oil is good for cooking chicken, but putting it on someone's head and leaving a big greasy mark is something different.

"Close your eyes, son, and put your hands up," he ordered.

"Uh oh, here we go," I thought to myself, cause I know where this is about to go. As soon as he put the palm of his hand with the cooking grease onto my head, he used a little force. I stood my ground though, because I refused to let him push me down this time. He got down on me before, and all the girls in the church were laughing at me. I got something for him this time.

"In the name of JESUS," he yelled "JESUS" out loud as he used a little more force than he did the first time. I started smiling because he was really trying hard and after about five minutes or so he finally gave up and ended the long winded prayer. I looked up at my grandmother and she was shaking her head. I know what she was thinking, and I know she knew what I was thinking and trying to prove.

I went back to my seat in the choir stand and my auntie slapped me across the head.

"What you do that for, boy? Don't play dumb with me....You knew what you were doing?" she whispered in my ear. I started laughing because not only did my grandma peep the play I put down, but so did everybody else. These preachers be killing me, but hey, I guess I gotta' go to Heaven, or maybe Hell. At least I have options I suppose, but whatever happened to the third option? It's always a, b, or c, but when you're in church it's just Heaven or Hell.

Looking out of the window I'm beginning to think that maybe there is a third option, and that there is something on the other side of the street where the grass is greener or is it just dye?

I've noticed that there are a lot of people who enjoy life all week long and are happy. They don't even go to church, but yet and still they live a prosperous life. They have all types of money in their pockets, different cars lined up in their driveway, and not to mention every new Jordan sneaker that comes out on their feet. Man, I'd do anything for a pair of

Jordans'. I know for a fact that they've gotta feel more comfortable than these church shoes.

I've even seen the pastor with a pair on at the church picnic. The older ones laugh at me often because I have a penny stuck in the tongue of mine. My mom picked these up from Payless Shoes before we came up here, and I've been forced to wear them ever since. My grandma says I better wear the sole out before I get another pair.

By the time church was over, I knew we were going to stay and eat. It was no telling how long my grandma was going to stay. I looked out the window and saw my cousin Tim standing outside his truck, across the street at the store. I walked out and went over to him. He was talking on his phone to somebody that had just walked past him.

"What's up, lil' cuz'?"

"What's up, Tim? What you doing out here?"

"Aww, nephew, I'm out here doing what needs to be done, you know. I see you still doing your church thing."

"Man, you know grandma is not going to let me miss a Sunday, Monday, Tuesday, Thur—"

"Yeah, yeah, I already know." He started laughing, "Where's your momma?"

"She couldn't make it. The last time I saw her she was with her sisters."

"Oh, so they must've gone out last night."

"Probably so."

"I wonder why she ain't called me. Hold on, wait a minute cuz." Somebody was walking up.

Tim stopped him in his tracks and I stepped off to the side. He pulled something out his pocket, gave the man a five, and then put his hand back in his pocket. Looking across the street I'm hoping that my grandma don't come out yelling, looking for me. One time she did. She yelled for like three minutes outside, and I was in the church the whole time. So embarrassing.

The people on the streets seem to have the answers to many of the problems.

"Cuz."

About a year ago, I was walking down the street and found a CD alongside the curb. It was turned upside down and it had a few scratches on it. I turned it over and it was a rap cd. I hadn't listened to rap before that point, and was eager to find out what rap was all about. My mom would never buy me any music because she said that the music that we sung in the church should last me the whole week, and asking my grandmother was completely out the question. I guess with all week long choir practices, singing at bible study, and at church on Sundays, she was right. I really didn't have time to listen to any new music in between.

Once I put the CD in the player I sat down in front of it and turned the speaker up to the max. I didn't move an inch. He had my undivided attention. I came across this song "Blasphemy." When I listened to it, my mind was captivated. It took my thoughts out of the hemisphere, and I began to think about how I fit into the equation. I often heard my grandma tell me to never use the Lord's name in vain because it's blasphemy, so the name of the song stood out to me the most.

At the beginning of the song it talked about Jesus coming back, and about God sending his son. This was the same thing that they preach about in church, but this guy, on the other hand, was making it sound so much better than the preacher did. My spirit was just as lifted as those that were in church. Could this be how people outside of church feel when I see them from the inside? I don't know, but if it is, I love it!

He quoted this lyric about us already being in Hell, and we don't even know it. What came to mind is that in church they tell you that Hell is full of fire, where you burn for eternity, but from the words of this guy, it sounds like he's doing the right kind of teaching that I can gain a better understanding of by not trying to spook me out. It was like a message in its most raw form. I began bobbing my head and taking it all in as I listened to it time and time again.

"Cuz"

"Huh…oh my bad Tim. What's up?"

"You day dreamin'?"

I started laughing because I was completely in a trance.

"What you looking at? He said while looking in the same direction that I was. It was a woman dancing to some music coming out of the speaker of this huge truck and people throwing dice around on the ground. I had never seen that many people play monopoly at the same time before. They got real money though, and instead of the monopoly board they have a piece of cardboard on the ground.

"Look around cuz," Tim put his arm around me. "It's a different world out here in these streets homie. It's safe in the church, and ain't nothing wrong with that. But out here, you gotta' move with the rest of them."

"What you mean by that?" I turned and looked at him.

"You gotta be a moving reality."

"A moving reality?" I was confused.

"Yeah, a moving reality. You gotta' focus on what's real." He pulled out a wad of money. "You need this."

"Whoa! Where did you get all this money?" He put the knot in my hand.

"I got it from the real world, from everything you see outside of church. You gotta' stop taking everything you hear or see in the church for face value. You gotta'—"

"Currrtis," my grandmother was yelling for me.

Sherrad O'Neil Glosson

"I'm over here," I hollered back.

She turned towards my direction. "Boy, get over here," she yelled.

"Alright, Tim," I gave him a five, he left a one hundred dollar bill in my hand and I ran back across the street.

As soon as I approached her, she started pulling my ear. "Ouch grandma. What you do that for?"

"Who told you to go across the street to the store?"

"I was talking to Tim."

She looked across the street and Tim was giving someone a five as they approached him. She just shook her head. Before I was halfway in the door of the church I turned around and looked back across the street. Tim was in his truck and it was smoking again. It was at that point that I came to grips that maybe it's not his car that's smokin' after all.

Life Starts When The Church Ends

CHAPTER 8

Riding down the street from my house I saw my mom running out of Uncle Charlie's house again. I don't know what or whom she was running from, but it looked like she was in a hurry. We pulled up to the curb and my grandmother didn't even bother to get out the car. She just honked the horn twice and I got out. My mom then came out to the porch and waved, as grandma was halfway out the driveway.

"Hey, Ma."

"Hey, son of mine, how are you doin'?" She hugged me and kissed me on the cheek.

"I'm fine, now that I'm home. Can I go play?"

"Yeah, but go and change your clothes first."

"Kay!" I said running in the house. Moments later, I came back outside and headed towards Gooney's.

"She ain't there, Young Buck."

I turned around and it was Uncle Charlie sitting on the porch, drinking some water, and smoking a cigar.

"You know where she went?"

"She'll be back soon. Come here for a minute, Young Buck. Let me talk to you for a sec."

I walked over to his porch and sat across from him.

"You know I appreciate you running those packages for me across the neighborhood. My legs have been really bad lately, and you have been a big help. Now listen, I have something for you. Can you run another one for me? It's a bit bigger than the other ones, so I'ma' need you to be careful with it. Okay?"

I nodded my head. "Can I ask you something? What's in these packages that I've been carrying? I've been doing this for a while and I've never looked inside."

He took a sip of water straight from the bumpy face bottle. "Candy."

"Candy!" I replied.

"Yeah, candy. But never mind that. Right now, I need you to take this to the store on Schafer, and tell the Arab guy behind the counter that Charlie sent you. Okay?"

I nodded my head to the instructions, but at the same time I'm thinking about the time when the Crips jumped me at the same store. Not only that, but if my mom sees me at the store without her permission again she might kill me. He gave me a duffle bag this time, and it was a bit heavier than the rest of the ones I used to carry.

"Make sure you come right back alright?" He stood up and walked in the house. I picked up the bag and headed to my house. I figured that I'll ask my mom if I could go to the store this time before she starts looking for me. I threw the bag on the side of the porch and went into the house.

"Hey ma, I yelled, running to the back of the house. Ma."

"I'm in here." She was in the laundry room.

"Can I go to the store, please?"

"With who?"

"With uh…"

"Uh…" she mocked me.

"Gooney."

"Yeah okay. Don't be long. As a matter of fact, I'm going with ya'll. Go grab my keys."

"No! Uh..go with us for what? We can handle ourselves."

"Now you know what happened the last time you went to the store."

"Yeah Ma, but that was a long time ago."

"And?" she said as she folded her arms.

"Annndd…come on, Ma. Can I go by myself? Please?" I tried to make her give in.

"By yourself? I thought Gooney was going with you?"

"Oh, she is. She went to get some money from her mom," I smiled.

"Okay, Curtis. You make sure ya'll come right back, and I mean right back. You hear me?"

I nodded my head and rushed back outside. I ran straight to where I threw the bag and it wasn't there. My heart began to beat fast and sweat was starting to pour down my face as I paced back and forth with my hands on my forehead. I didn't wanna' go and tell Uncle Charlie that somebody stole his bag, but I guess it's better to say something now as opposed to later. I walked over to his doorstep.

"Young Buck!" He yelled before I could even knock.

"I have something to tell you."

"Something like what? You left something on the side of the house, and you thought somebody stole it?" He came to the door with the duffle bag.

"Uncle Charlie, I—"

"Let me guess, you went home to ask yo' momma can you go to the store huh?"

I nodded my head in agreement.

"Look here, Young Buck. Sometimes when it's business on the floor you gotta' separate family from business. It's something like water and oil. You know what I mean?"

I just looked at him waiting to explain.

"Have you ever seen water and oil in the same place at the same time?"

"Yeah"

"What happens when they mix?"

I looked at the ground trying to figure out where he was going with this. "They don't."

"That's right, Young Buck. Even though this world is built of oil and water you need water to live, and oil to survive. You gotta' understand that you are the oil. People go to church because they need some type of order, or they feel they need some structure. They want to know how to live, but once they leave the church building and come to the real world, what do you see people choosing?"

"The oil."

"Exactly, you see America fighting for it every day. That's what this country is about. This country is a junkie, and the oil is the fix. You'll understand sooner or later young Buck, just remember to never leave something like this just lying around? He gave me the bag and I headed to the store.

I thought to myself, "what does he mean by being the oil?" It's always a metaphor that I can't figure out. I guess it's something that I'll understand as I get older.

When I got to the store it wasn't anyone around. I walked in and went straight to the counter. An Arab was talking on the phone. When he saw me coming, he started speaking in Arabic. His head is covered up and he smelled like pickles and hot mustard for some reason. He looked at me, and then put his hand over the mic of the phone.

"Hello, my friend."

"Uncle Charlie sent me."

He looked down at the duffle bag, and then at the door. "Where is he, my friend?"

"Back at home."

"And he sent you? What are you his son or something?"

"He told me to bring this to you."

He went back to talking on the phone and moments later hung up.

"Go put the closed sign on the door" he ordered.

I walked over to the door, looked out the window to see if anyone was coming, and turned back to him.

"Hurry, buddy, hurry!" He motioned his hands.

I turned the sign over, and followed him to the back of the store. "Follow me, buddy."

When we walked in the back room, two guys were sitting at a table smoking cigars. They looked Italian, like they were part of the mob or something.   They looked at me crazy; tryna' figure out what I was doing there, and then noticed the duffle bag.

"Where is Charlie?" One of them asked the Arab who brought me in.

"He sent him."

The two Italians looked at each other and I was just as confused and a little paranoid at the same time.

"Gimme," one of them motioned for the bag.

I walked over to him and handed him the bag.

"How do you know Charlie?"

"He's my neighbor."

"Your neighbor, huh?" Do you know what's in here?" he unzipped it.

"Uncle Charlie told me candy."

"Candy!" They all started laughing, like I just told a joke that I was the only one that didn't get it.

"Yeah, he told me it was candy."

"What do you mean? Like Now and Laters, Jolly Ranchers, what?" They started laughing again.

He pulled a zip lock bag out of it that looked like it was either the pure sugar that my mom uses for making Kool-Aid, or the flour she uses to make pork chops. He pulled a knife out his pocket and cut one of the packages down the middle. Stuck the tip of the knife in it, and pulled it back out with some of the white substance on it. Stuck his tongue out and put the tip of his tongue on the end of the knife. Then he immediately made a sound as he jumped back, as if it had burned him.

"This is 100% coke," he said.

I looked at him still dumbfounded.

"How long you been doing this for Charlie?"

"For a couple of years."

"A couple of years huh? And you never looked inside."

I nodded my head. "Well, what is coke?"

"It's the answer to all your problems my friend. But you're only a teen, so you don't have any problems yet. This is every Jordan sneaker that you ever wanted my friend," the Arab chimed in.

I looked at the coke trying to understand how I've been running these packages through the neighborhood not knowing what was in them until now. I'm wondering how this can be every Jordan sneaker that I always wanted. I've always thought that this was sugar or the powder that my mom buys to make food and drink with. Now, I'm hearing that this is the answer to all my problems.

"So this ain't sugar or powder?"

They looked at each other, and seconds later they started laughing again. The Arab thought it was too funny because he was rolling around on the floor in laughter.

"It's cocaine my friend."

"Cocaine huh?" I was too confused and was ready to get back to Uncle Charlie so he could explain. "Are we done?"

"Oh yeah, my friend. You can leave now."

I headed back through the way I had just come.

"Hey, youngsta'." I turned around. "What's your name?"

"Bird"

He nodded his head. "Tell Charlie to call me okay?"

I nodded and headed out the store. I couldn't wait to get to Charlie's house. As soon as I ran back towards home I saw my mom standing on the porch smoking a cigarette. Gooney was sitting on the side of her, and I knew I was in a lot of trouble.

"Curtis, you betta get your lil' tail up here right now!" She yelled. "Where the hell were you?" She grabbed me by the arm as I approached her.

"At the store."

"I thought Gooney was going with you. She over here looking for you when ya'll supposed to be together. As a matter of fact, don't answer that. Get in this house. You gonna' get your lil' behind whooped this afternoon." She smacked me in the back of my head.

Uncle Charlie was sitting on the porch watching the whole thing.

"Go get a switch off that tree, and you better pick out a good one."

I walked over to the trees, grabbed a branch, and walked over to Charlie's with a confused look on my face. I knew he knew something.

"Coke?" I asked.

"Life starts when the church ends, Young Buck." He smiled before taking a sip of his drink.

"Cuurrrtis! Get your lil' behind in here!"

Life Starts When The Church Ends

CHAPTER 9

2 years later…

We are all a bit older now, attending the same high school. Ecorse high school, of course. We are still as tight as we have always been. All of us have gone through some changes and we have experienced life in the many forms it has to offer.

My grandma still make me go to church every Sunday, but it's not the same anymore. I'm finding myself outside of church, and contrary to what I've been taught throughout my life, I'm flipping work now and making a lil money for myself. Every since I found out that Uncle Charlie had me running drugs across the neighborhood for him, and making a profit, I figured I'd run my own drugs and make more money cutting out the middleman. Uncle Charlie didn't mind that I had stopped doing it for him because he said I was going to catch on sooner or later. He told me that I was too naive about how the world outside of church operated, and that I had to learn as I got older.

Well, I guess he knew what he was talking about because I'm banking at least five to six hundred dollars a week. At fourteen, that's damn near better than what the average family makes working a nine to five. Sometimes, I'll be in church not even paying attention at all, and I'll be in my choir seat making sells. Hell, it ain't like singing in the choir is keeping my gear tight. They take money from you by making you pay tithes. I really wish that I had my own place, that way I'd be making more money, and I could come to church whenever I wanted. I could come on my own, and as much money as I'm making now I'll have my own place in no time. I bought me a Chevy though and you already know me and my crew be rolling around the hood. My homeboy hooked me up with some twelve inch sub woofers, and I bought some twenties from this crack-head that I got for one rock per rim. Yep, I got 'em good, but dope fiends will do anything just to get a high.

I found out that my mom was working for Uncle Charlie. I was driving down Schafer one night with Buck, and I saw her on the corner with some fishnet pantyhose, some red leather heels, and a shirt to match. She was walking up to Uncle Charlie's car giving him some money. It shocked the hell outta' me the first time I saw it, but I didn't mention it to her. It did do a number on me though. Everybody's gotta' get money somehow, and if that's how she got to get hers, then so be it. I can't knock her hustle.

Buck started doing drugs, smoking weed, poppin' pills like crazy. He'd sell a little something here and there, but he's getting money too. Of course, that's if he don't smoke it all up. At times he'll just make a little something to smoke.

I found out that Gooney has been stripping for parties and has been doing it for a minute now. I was looking for her one night and Uncle Charlie was on his porch. He said that she'd be back in a minute. I thought about when I was younger and he would say the same thing. Come to find out, he had her dancing at parties since we were kids. Gooney finally told me that she had been doing that since we were younger. Now, she's stripping for a local club. She's been getting paid too, and people around here respect her, and not only her, but also the crew as a whole. Everybody understands that we are ready to go to war for each other.

Mike and his brother, Ike, turned into hit men. They even made a name for themselves in the streets and are known as the Motor City Hitters. They are reckless too, and will put anybody down for whatever reason.

We all pretty much ventured off into other things, but one thing we have and will always have in common is loyalty. That's something that's rare in the city of Detroit. People will turn on you in a heartbeat, family or not. These fools around here are straight snakes. Uncle Charlie once told me that just because a snake may not be venomous or have teeth doesn't mean that you can get close to it and try to make it a pet. He's still a snake. Uncle Charlie always dropped some cold jewels on me, and yet there's still one that I haven't cracked open yet.

Come to find out, my cousin Tim was moving the bag for a minute as well. I can't believe that fool had me thinking that his car really needed an oil change when he was smoking in it. He smoke just as much as Snoop Dogg. He's been on the run for a minute because his house got raided, and they found some scales, three pounds of weed, and two choppas with the clips half empty. They tryna' link him to a house that was shot up on 7th street. He went down to Virginia with our older cousins. He say them boys down there are really getting paper. I'm gonna' have to go and check that out myself once I get my weight up.

It's crazy because I was once asked, "How did I end up like this?" I was born in the church, going to church every single day of the week, and singing in the choir. I should have a one-way ticket to Heaven. I thought about it for a minute, but didn't really need to think about it that hard. I felt like that being always taught the Bible, and constantly being preached to about Heaven and Hell, didn't help me with real life problems.

All they were doing was telling me stories from the bible about a man who had blonde hair and blue eyes. That's not how he's described in the bible, but how you'll see him hanging in the church. I mean, who's going to tell me about what's going on in the world today as opposed to what went on back then. That's something that I always wanted my father to teach me, but unfortunately he wasn't around. So, where does that leave me? Learning from my environment?

I guess if the whole world was a sanctuary it would be a peaceful world, but you still have people running up in churches, shooting and killing people, and preachers coming out of the closet. I'm not going to mention any names but if you follow these so-called pastors and gospel singers you know exactly who I'm talking about. It was the people I looked up to, but once I realized that church wasn't all that it was cracked up to be, I found out that the streets were the realest thing. I've learned that the streets are your greatest teacher.

It was a must that I get a gun because I don't think a knife would be that sufficient if you always in the streets hustling. Good thing I haven't had any problems and everybody pretty much respects me. Sometimes I think about how one little act of bravery as a kid paved the way for respect years down the line.

The day I pulled that knife out on those bullies had people skeptical about picking with me because they didn't know what to expect from me. Now that I carry a gun, you can just imagine how people don't even flinch when I come through. I guess you can say the church raised me, but the streets made me. Funny, when I was younger, my mom and I used to watch New York Undercover every week and now I own a Glock.

"What's up, Buck?" I said getting out of the car.

"What's up, Bird? What's good? Why you in all red?"

"This is what it is now."

"Bloods?"

"It's just my favorite color, and I wouldn't mind running into those Crips to piss them off. Where is everyone?"

"Mike and Ike should be coming out in a minute."

"Hey ya'll!" Gooney came out the door wearing a blue scarf around her head.

"What is that on your head?" I asked her.

"Boy, I'm not trying have my hair all messed up and all over the place. I just got it done yesterday."

"Well, put this on." I pulled out a red scarf and gave it to her. "Here." I took the blue rag from her, tore it up in pieces, and threw it on the ground. Mike and Ike came out and met us on the sidewalk.

It's the first day of school, and it feels good to be starting high school. Middle school went by pretty fast. My mom doesn't know about me selling drugs or holding guns. If she did, she'd probably beat me into a new day. I ain't trippin' though because we stay in the projects and the way I see it, you either get with it or YOU WILL be it.

"Ya'll ready to go?"

"You really wanna' go to school on the first day?" Gooney asked as we got in the car and started rolling.

"Yeah, why not? We ain't been in school all summer, and I know it's some new booty up in there."

"Ugh, right." She rolled her eyes.

"It's a ditch party today too," Ike chimed in.

"On the first day?" Buck asked.

"Yep, are ya'll going?"

They all looked at me waiting on me to give the okay to go. "Watcha' looking at me for? Oh I guess ya'll waiting on me, huh?"

They nodded their heads as if it wasn't even a question to be answered.

"Where is it?"

"It's on Joy Road and Braile."

"All the way on the west side and the deep west side at that?"

I thought about it for a minute because I really wanted to go to school at least on the first day, but what the hell. I'm with it.

"Let's ride!"

Buck pulled out a blunt that he rolled up before he came outside, and as soon as he lit it the smell of California Cush wreaked throughout the car.

Life Starts When The Church Ends

CHAPTER 10

When we got to the party there were a few cars outside. We all were fried out our brains and had stopped at a few gas stations to get some snacks on the way. Ain't nothing like a fifty-cent juice and some Little Debbie's to chase a high. Buck rolled up another blunt, but he'll probably be smoking that one on his own. Once I get high I'm usually good. I don't feel like I can get any higher after that point. Buck, on the other hand, will smoke and keep smoking until he falls asleep. It's like his NyQuil or something.

We got out the car and walked towards the house. We heard a little music. "They must be really happy that school started 'cause they jammin' like it's midnight," said Gooney.

Knock, knock, knock!

This female opened the door.

"What's up?"

"You tell me." I replied back.

She looked at me and my crew, and we're standing there feeling high as a kite in the middle of fall.

"Hold on wait! Ain't ya'll them twin boys they call Motor City Hitters?" She said looking at Mike and his brother behind us.

"Yeah, and, so?"

"Oh, ya'll can't come in here."

"Why not?" I asked.

"Ya'll not about to start no trouble up in here. I'm sorry."

"Man, we just came to have a good time, baby, that's all. So quit tripping," I replied.

"Soorrryy…" she rolled her eyes and popped her gum.

"Alright look," I stopped her from closing the door in my face. "How about I pay you?"

"I'm listenin'," she folded her arms.

I pulled out a wad of money and gave her five hundred dollars. "Here's a few hundred dollars for all of us. Now, can we get in?"

She stepped off to the side and we walked in.

"You should have let me snatch that ponytail out her head," Gooney said pissed off.

"It's cool. We in here now, but you betta' believe if we didn't get in it was going down, and she would've paid me for some gas money."

We started laughing.

"I'm about to go over here." Buck said walking off to the side somewhere.

There were quite a few people in here for it to be a ditch party. Gooney, Mike, Ike and I went downstairs to where the music was coming. Why is it that at every house party people are always trying look hard, knowing that they can't move nothing? All eyes were on us as we walked through the crowd. We found a corner, and created our own lil' cipher. Mike pulled out some liquor and we passed it around, taking a sip. I remember when I was younger, Uncle Charlie used to drink this same stuff. I thought it was water though, but come to find out it's the life of the party.

"Let me get some," Buck said meeting us in the corner.

"Where were you at?"

"I saw a snack table. You know I had to get my munch on."

We were having a good time and all the guys were trying to get Gooney to dance. She wasn't having it though, and of course, all the females was hatin' on her. One girl said she knew her and was telling people that she was a stripper and a hood rat. Gooney didn't care though cause she was used to the attention, and she actually loved it.

"Watch this," Gooney said giving me her purse.

A song by New York rapper came on called 'Killin'em,' and she went to the middle of the floor and started dancing. People from upstairs was hearing all the guys yelling "oooh" and started coming downstairs to see what was going on. She was putting on a show, and we in the corner loving every minute of it.

"That's my baby right there!" I yelled giving her a boost.

She took her shirt off and put it on the floor, turned upside down in a hand stand, using her hands as balance, and was popping her butt. "Oooohh," she had the crowd going, and we in the corner clownin' throwing money at her. Everybody else followed suit.

One of the girls went and turned off the music, and Gooney was still upside down. We started giving her a beat with our hands and she continued her performance. We bursted out laughing cause she just shut the party down and she knew it.

"Booyah!" Gooney said getting up, walking over to us with all the money in her hand. We were hyped by then because everywhere we go, we clown, and Gooney just shuts it down completely.

I was sitting there thinking for a minute and it dawned on me that I spent five hundred dollars just for us to get in here.

"Man, I let this chick get down on us." I said to myself but loud enough for others to hear.

"Who? Watchu' talkin' 'bout?" Mike asked.

"The girl I gave five hundred dollars to…I'm gonna' need that back. Let's go."

We all headed upstairs looking for ole girl, and she was nowhere in sight. I'm mad as hell, not to mention the weed and liquor I got in my system. Liquor boils at 120° and it don't take that long to get pissed off so I'm heated right now.

"Hey girl!" I yelled as I saw her in the kitchen. "I need my money back."

"What?"

"You heard me. You made me pay five hundred just to get in this damn party, and it's whack. My girl had to shut it down just to get it jumping in here. Now, I want my money back or else."

She stood there for a minute and then conformed to the configuration.

"We out man." I said once she gave us the money back.

We were halfway to the car until I thought about how mad I was about that money.

"Hold on a minute." I pulled out my Glock and stood in front of the house. Blahgah…click-click-click-click!! I forgot that I only keep one bullet in the chamber because it was for emergency purposes only. Gooney was cracking up behind me because she knew I only had one bullet in it.

"What are you doing?" Gooney said still cracking up.

"I forgot. Let's go man." I said running back to the car.

We drove down Joy Road to the Southfield freeway, and headed back to our side of Detroit. I had to stop by my spot house just to see if people were doing what was supposed to be done. I got a couple of people from school that I've known since middle school holding things down.

When I walked up to the door, I had to give them the test to see if they were on point.

149

I knocked once, kicked the door twice, and then knocked once again.

"Is that it?" someone on the other side yelled.

"One twenty-one," I yelled and he opened the door.

"What's up, boy?" He greeted me as I came in.

"What's up? We gettin' money?"

"Aww, you already know what it is." He pulled out some cash.

"Okay, okay, you getting' it."

"Where yo' cousin at?"

"He went to the store right quick. He should be on his way back now."

"How much more product ya'll got left?"

"It's about time to re-up now, we on the last few ounces."

"Alright, bet."

"Bird," Gooney yelled. "It looks like those Crips that you got into it with a while ago."

"What? Where?"

She looked out the door. We all stepped outside, and they were at a house across the street, but a few doors down.

"Mike, you loaded?"

"Yeah, you know it."

"Let's ride," I said as we were walking across the street. I pulled out my pistol.

"What's up, Cuz?" I yelled, and they all turned around.

"Bird! Wait!" I heard Gooney yell.

Click click-click-click. "Dammit!" I forgot I didn't have any damn bullets.

They pulled out their pistols immediately and shots went off.

I went and grabbed Gooney and we ran behind the car.

Buck, Mike, and Ike were taking care of business until I heard someone yell.

They still kept shooting, but moments later it stopped. I poked my head out and saw that they had got in their cars and took off down the street. "Arrgggh!" Someone hollered, and I went to see who it was. Buck was on the ground rolling from side to side.

"Buck, what's up?" I ran to him.

"I got shot in the foot. Arrgggh! Don't touch me, bro!"

He was holding his foot as blood was dripping from his shoe.

"Man, I just bought these shoes."

We all started laughing as he was in pain.

"What's so funny? I'm hurt!"

"Man, you ain't hurt fool. Get up," Gooney said.

I stood there happy that nothing major happened, because if it was more serious than this I would've been the one to blame. I went to a damn gunfight without any bullets! Where they do that at?

Sherrad O'Neil Glosson

Life Starts When The Church Ends

CHAPTER 11

MODERN DAY

I've been in the hole for about ten days and it's really starting to get under my skin. The guards are acting like they don't want to feed me, so they keep bringing me food loafs instead. A food loaf is when food is put into a blender and baked like a loaf of bread. And trust me when I say this, it's not the best meal on the market to eat. I haven't really eaten anything since I've been in here, and I know I've lost at least forty pounds by now. My body is so weak that every time I move I feel like I'm about to pass out. I just lie down, stare at the darkness, and let my mind take me wherever it wants to go.

I imagine that thought's travel at twenty-four billion miles per second, so you know my mind is all over the place. I wonder where I went wrong and how I ended up in this position. I've been in the church since I was a baby, and my grandma made sure I was there every day, even during the week. I sung in the choir and even prayed from time to time. If I was doing all of this, why is God punishing me like this?

I remember Jesus even crying out to his own father why did he forsake him. I mean, on one hand, you have preachers out here preaching up a storm in the pulpit, and on the hand getting charged for molesting boys. Trust me, I've seen it with my own eyes. So why is it me? Not even a vessel of God is being severely punished. I guess He will forsake His own, just like He did His own son.

Jesus was being crucified and asked His dad why He was doing this. So just think, if God sent His own son to death, His own son, why should or would He care about me? We're not even related. I know I ain't walking around healing the blind and doing work like Him. I'm just a black man living in the United States of America, who has been oppressed and expected to be nothing in this world. The court is tryna' crucify me and hand me my own cross. They got a rope around my neck, and the only thing I'm standing on is a glass bottle.

Facing time in prison is like death in a sense. Once you die, people will weep over you for a moment, but as time goes on, their tears begin to fade away and you are no longer a memory or even a thought. You are in a place other than your own, and you gotta' survive on someone else's turf.

"Books"

"Huh?"

"Your lawyer is here to see you. Get up."

The guard came and opened the cell gate. I haven't seen my lawyer since I had that court appointed lawyer that was tryna' nail me to the wall. My mom didn't say that she found a paid attorney either.

"Let's go, Books, he don't have all day," he yelled as I was slowly getting up. He handcuffed me from the front, grabbed my arm, and led me down the hallway.

"In here" He opened the door, "Your lawyer will be in here in a minute. Have a seat."

I sat down on the steel metal table that had two seats across from each other. I'm guessing that this is the lawyer my mom got for me. The door opened and a short male walked in wearing one of those hats that has a flimsy brim around it. The brim was really low, covering half his face, reminding me of Dick Tracy or somebody. I stood up to shake his hand.

"Sit down, kid." He said while taking his hat off.

It was the Italian that I had met at the liquor store when I was running those packages for Uncle Charlie.

"What are you doing here?"

"I'm here to help you."

"Did Uncle Charlie send you to come here to see me?"

"Kid, you're asking too many questions already. That's my job. I'm here to get you off this case."

"Oh yeah, And how you gonna' do that? They got a gun, bodies, and me."

"Look at me kid. LOOK AT ME! I know people who know people. All you gotta' do is what I say do, and what I tell you to say."

"How much is it going to cost?"

"Now, you're asking the right question. If and when we beat this case, and we save you from spending the rest of your life behind bars, you are going to work for me. I like how you do work. I observed you back at the store. I can use somebody like you on my team. All you gotta' do is help me to help you."

It sounds promising. At the same time, how could I give up this offer? I heard a poet say, 'It's Heaven or Hell, freedom or jail." I don't know of anyone who wouldn't choose freedom over spending the rest of his or her life behind the wall.

"You've got a tough case, kid. The evidence I see doesn't look too good on your part," He said while flipping through my file. "And by the way, kid, if you didn't commit the crime, how did they find gun powder on your fingers? As a matter of fact, don't answer that. Everyone is innocent until proven guilty right?"

"Well, if that's the case then, why am I still in jail?" I stood up yelling in rage.

"Look, kid," he held up my file, "You have an armed robbery, two 1st degree murders, the murder weapon and gun powder on your hands. You think they gonna' just let you out onto the streets so you can run? You're a flight risk. It don't work like that, kid, so sit down and listen."

I guess he was right. I'm facing a hard case, and I needed all the help I could get.

"Think about it and I'll be back up here in a bit." He stood up and we shook hands. "Why do you look so pitiful kid?"

"I'm in the hole."

"The hole, for what?"

"I was in a fight. This white boy stole some of my commissary."

"Well, did you win?" He started laughing. "Just joking, kid, lighten up. I'll take care of that. Hey, guard!" he yelled.

 Moments later the guard came and opened the door. "Get my client outta' the hole will you? He's getting sick in there."

The guard took the cuffs off me and took me out the room.

"Aye, kid."

I turned around. "Charlie told me to tell ya' life starts when the church ends."

Life Starts When The Church Ends

CHAPTER 12

CHURCH

"Please turn your Bibles to Hebrews 5 starting at verse 11.

May we all stand for the reading of His word."

The preacher started with his sermon of the day.

"So it reads in the New International Version starting at verse 11: We have so much to say about this, but it is hard to make it clear to you because you no longer try to understand.

Vs 12: in fact, though by this time you ought to be teachers, you need someone to teach you the elementary truths of Gods word all over again. You need milk, not solid food.

Vs 13: anyone who lives on milk, being still an infant, is not acquainted with the teaching about righteousness.

Vs 14: but solid food is for the mature, who by constant use have trained themselves to distinguish good from evil.

I want to talk to you all about something that's been on my heart for a while now. I've been hearing different saints with different issues regarding the way I handle certain situations with other saints. What I don't understand is how we can complain about our problems day in and day out all day on social media, but we won't take our problems to God. We value the opinions of others but we don't value the promises of God's word which is far more valid than any opinion we can hear from another human being. Why do we think we want more but we can only handle less? The scripture says we can't handle meat because we aren't mature enough and we can only drink milk because we are babes. We think we are grown because of our age, but I have news for you. You are not grown. Some of us are forty five years old still playing twenty year old games and we wonder why we still aren't married.

Many of you are acting just like babies. When a baby's teeth start to come in, it will cry and seek attention until someone helps provide comfort. Just like in the spiritual world, you start coming to church and you get a little word in you and you get saved. After a while, the high of being saved starts to wear off. You feel like you need some attention so you start creating havoc and start raising hell in the church. You're not grown. When you're grown, you have permanent teeth and can handle meat, people talking about you, and people always being negative toward you. You're not a baby so you don't need anyone to constantly feed you or watch you just in case you get into trouble. You all are mature and can make things happen on your own."

I came to church pretty late because we all went out last night. I haven't even been to choir practice all week. I know my grandma gonna' be tripping on me as soon as service is over. I still have a hangover and I still reek of marijuana too. I shouldn't even go in, but hell, I'm here now, so it is what it is.

When I walked up to the door they were praying, and I knew I wasn't about to go in right then. They weren't about to have me in here smelling like dead grass in Texas. They might throw the whole bottle of anointing oil on me.

I walked across the street to the store to waste some time. When I walked in, someone was mopping the floor in the back and there was a Chaldean woman behind the register.

"Excuse me," she called me.

"What's up?"

"Are you going to buy anything?"

"What you got a problem with me being here or something?"

She looked at the guy in the back to see if he was paying attention.

"What you looking at him for?"

"I'm sorry but you can't stand in here unless you're buying something."

"Alright, alright…Look, let me get a shot of tequila."

"Is that it?"

"Damn, do you want me to buy something else?"

I gave her the money. "Keep the change. It looks like you could use it anyway."

I went back to the spot where I was standing before she interrupted me, took the shot of tequila right there, and threw the bottle on the ground. I don't know how long I was standing there but I was in a zone. That shot has me drunk again. I forgot why I was standing there in the first place. "Oh yeah, I was going to church."

I started laughing because my mind was gone just that quick. She might have even spiked my shot before she gave it to me. "But wait!" I opened it myself. I busted out laughing again as I was walking across the street, headed back to church.

Before I opened the door, I checked to make sure my clothes were straight. I had on a three-piece grey suit with some Stacy Adams shoes. I looked in the window, and everyone was seated. I opened the door and walked in.

"Good morning, Brother Books."

"Hey, how you doing, Mother Louis?"

"I'm fine. You going into the choir stand?"

167

"Oh no, I'm gonna' sit back here today."

She started fanning me as if I smelled. I was hot so the little breeze that the fan was giving off did feel good. I closed my eyes and let her fan me.

"Do you know you smell like alcohol?"

"I do?" I opened my eyes paranoid.

She shook her head and put the fan over her nose to block the smell. I know I put some cologne on in the car before I came in, so I know I can't smell that bad. I went and sat in the back of the church by the fan. I was so hot that I needed more than the church fans they hand out. I sat right in front of the floor fan and then tuned in to the service.

I was looking for my grandma but didn't see her around. She's usually sitting in the choir to the right of the preacher. I didn't even see her Bible or her briefcase.

"Hey, Mother Louis," I called the usher over to me. "Where is my grandma?"

"I think she had to speak at another church service," she whispered.

That was even better, because now I don't have to hear her mouth about why I wasn't in choir practice. At least she'll know that I was at service. I smelled food coming through the vents from downstairs, and I was getting hungry. My body was so hot, and sitting in front of that fan felt so good that I didn't want to move. I wasn't even paying attention to what the preacher was saying. I was too busy enjoying my buzz. I can't believe I'm half drunk in church. I shouldn't have even come.

"Brother Books" someone called and I opened my eyes. "Brother Books, come give us some words." It was the preacher calling me.

"Huh?" I asked with a puzzled look as everybody turned towards me.

"Yeah, come tell us a little something about the blood of Jesus. Just a little testimony, that's all."

The church started clapping. "Alright now," someone yelled.

In the back of my head I'm like "you gotta' be kiddin' me. Is God punking me right now?"

"Yeah son," someone yelled, and for a second I thought they were hearing my thoughts. I stood up and proceeded to walk toward the front of the congregation. Good thing I didn't have to go to the pulpit, but I still had to stand at the podium that was off to the side. I pounded the mic to make sure it was on. "Can ya'll hear me?"

"Tell it!" someone yelled.

I was nervous as all outdoors, not to mention I was standing in front of God's people on cloud nine. I took a deep breath, sighed, then said the first thing I know...

"God is good."

"All the time," they replied back.

"And all the time."

"God is good," they replied again.

I'm trying to figure out how rappers smoke weed while they are in the booth. I can't even think straight. I thought about what my uncle used to say down south that got the people revved up.

"When I think of His goodness, and all that He's done for me. My soul cries out Hallelujah!' I thank God for saving me."

"You betta tell preach!" someone yelled as my plan worked. From then on, I just went for what I know. "God forgive me," I said in the back of my head. I went on for about three minutes or so. I didn't even remember what I was saying. I know people were fanning me to death because I was sweating. Mother Louis was in the back holding her nose, shaking her head. I know she is going to tell my grandmother about this, and it ain't even my fault. The preacher shouldn't have put me on the spot in the first place.

"I'll leave ya'll with this."

"Leave it," someone yelled.

"One fish, two fish, red fish, blue fish, nic-nac, patty-whack give a dog a bone."

I looked up and everyone was silent, just staring at me. Looking at each other probably asking, "did he just say what we think he said?"

I gotta' stop watching all these movies when I smoke.

"Okay brother, that's enough." The preacher came from the pulpit and whispered in my ear.

I was so embarrassed I walked slowly down the aisle with my head down and my pores reeking of tequila.

CHAPTER 13

MODERN DAY

"Books, you got a visit." The guard came and unlocked the cell gate. I wonder who it could be. I know it ain't my mom or my cousin, Tim. I ain't even had a visit since I been here other than my attorney. I walked out of the cell and went into this little room that had three windows, with a hole in the middle of it covered with a screen. I thought it was going to be at least a contact visit. I sat down waiting on whomever was about to come.

"Bird," someone yelled as I had my head down. When I looked up it was Gooney and Buck.

"What's up, ya'll?" I was excited.

"What's up with you?"

"Man, I'm trying to get the hell outta' here. I was thinking about ya'll too, and ya'll just showed up out the blue."

"Man, you know we miss you" Gooney said.

"Where Mike and Ike at?"

"You know they ain't coming up in here. All the bodies they got."

"Shhhh," I suggested. "You gotta' keep that low in here. These fools in here telling left and right. "You know we've been looking for that fool who did this right?" Buck said.

"Straight up! I can't wait 'til I see him again."

"I know man. We've been searching high and low for him and he ain't nowhere to be found. Mike and Ike haven't heard anything either."

"What they say they gon' do?" Gooney asked.

"I don't know yet. The court appointed lawyer was trying book me, so I had to get a paid one."

"How much?"

"It's already taken care of. Ya'll been by the spot?"

"Everyday. Everything is everything. You ain't gotta' worry. You know we got you. You been good in here?"

"I had a little problem with this white boy. I had to choke him out. He stole some of my Little Debbie's."

"Oh, we know how you like them Lil' Debbie's," Buck chimed in.

We all bursted out laughing. It felt good to laugh again, especially with my friends. They say this is the place where you find out who your friends really are. Either they're gonna' ride with you or fall by the wayside. Fortunately, mine are still holding me down.

"Gooney, got something to tell you."

"Oh yeah? What?"

"Nothing, he don't know what he talking about." She shot back, giving him the look.

"Tell him, what you scared of?"

"Tell me what?"

"I'll tell you when you get out. It won't be long."

"So, you ain't got no witness?" Buck asked.

"Man, all I got is my word against theirs and you know they trying to send me away forever! I can't believe I got caught up on some bullcrap like this." I shook my head.

"Well, if that raggedy car of yours would have started we wouldn't be in this position," Gooney joked.

We started laughing.

"It got us from point A to point B. Remember that time we went to that party over on Joy Road and that girl acted like she didn't wanna' let us in?

"Yeah, and you tried to shoot the house up with one bullet."

We bursted out laughing talking about old times, and for a split second I felt like I wasn't even in jail. It's a good feeling when you got support on the outside from your friends. You expect your family to have your back, but it ain't nothing like friends. I can say that me and my friends been through alot together, and been holding each other down, for real, since day one.

"I got to go to court again in about a week to see what's going to happen. I need ya'll to keep trying to find ole' boy so I can get up outta' here."

"We got you, homie. You already know, bro."

"I miss ya'll too, man."

"Jail making you back soft? What, you gon' go back to church when you get out too, huh?"

"Gooney, shut up," I laughed. "I'm serious though, ya'll my family and I miss ya'll, man."

"We miss you too, homie."

"You can say that again," Buck whispered.

"What you say?" I asked.

Gooney looked at him crazy like he better keep his mouth shut.

"Alright, visits over", the guard yelled over the intercom.

"Damn, we were only here for about fifteen minutes," Buck yelled back.

"I'll see ya'll later alright?" I put my hand on the glass.

"Boy, you watch too many movies," Gooney said putting her hand up to mine. I looked at Buck waiting on him to do the same.

"Aw, come on, bro. Are you serious?" He started laughing. "If it makes you feel better."

"Time to go," the guard yelled.

I got up and went back to my cell. When I got to my bunk, I just laid down with my thoughts floating in the air. I'm thinking about what I'm going to do to get out of this. Am I going to start living right and get back in the church? Or am I going to take on the new life that the streets made me. It really shouldn't even be a hard debate.

When you look at how my grandma forced me into the church and tried to make me into what she wanted me to be, compared to what the streets has made me, I would rather do what I wanted instead of what I was forced to do. I wonder if

I would kill Tom Tom if I saw him again. I really don't know too many people who wouldn't if they were in my position. I looked down and Cutty was reading a book.

"Aye, Cutty."

"What's up, youngsta'?"

"You know my case right?"

"Yeah, only what you told me."

"Let me ask you this. Would you get out and kill old boy if you had the chance? Or would you do what you know you're supposed to do?"

He closed the book and sat up on his bunk, "I can answer that in a simplistic way. It all depends on what you know you're supposed to do. If you feel like you are supposed to kill him on sight, then do it. I can't give you my point of view because I don't want you to base your actions off my way of thinking. But I will tell you this though, actions are judged by intentions. Actions may appear wrong, but motives bring rewards."

I didn't say another word after that. Although it was simplistic, it still had me thinking about what I was supposed to do. They say 'Men do what they want, and boys do what they can.' I guess I'll answer that question once I have the opportunity. Uncle Charlie always told me that I had to be an opportunist. The more I thought about the things he told me growing up, the more it clicked in my head. I'm still wondering why he said "life starts when the church ends."

CHAPTER 14

We just got out of school and we were sitting in the parking lot messing with everybody that was leaving late. We smoked in the gym locker room during our last period. The smoke was so thick it triggered the fire alarm. Buck had California's finest Cush again, and we were blowed out of our minds.

My cell phone was ringing, but I wasn't about to answer it because I knew it was my grandmother. I haven't talked to her since that day I was at church tripping. When I told my crew the story, they wanted to come to church the next time I went just to see if it would happen again. Gooney was falling all on the floor cracking up. It was funny, yet embarrassing, and I can't believe I went to church like that.

That's how you know when you too messed up, when you play with God. On the other hand, I guess I'm playing with God anyway because I'm doing the complete opposite of what I know I'm supposed to do. I remember when I was a kid and my grandfather asked me if I knew that I had a calling on my life. Without even thinking about it, I told him "no." I don't see why I've got to tell people about something that they can read for themselves. Willie Lynch said it best concerning us being ignorant and not reading. So what, I gotta' read for everybody else? I think not, therefore, I'm not. I don't understand why other preachers haven't had this notion yet. I guess some have. That's why they taking the congregation's money every week, talking about a building fund. Churches have been saying that for fifteen years but all they built was a bigger house.for the pastor.

"You don't hear no phone ringing?" Mike asked.

"It's my grandma."

"Oh, you know what she's gonna' say."

"Yeah, and I'm not trying to hear any of it either."

"Yeah, I wouldn't either. Aye, ya'll wanna' come with me to get my hair cut?" said Mike.

"Yeah. Where you going?"

"On 7th street."

"Oh, that's my man Rickie Jay, Let's ride."

Me, Gooney, Buck, Mike, and Ike got into the car and headed to Rickie Jay's on 7th. By the time we pulled up to his house he was already outside sitting on the porch.

"I've been waiting on ya'll since 3:05," he yelled looking at his watch. We walked up to the porch and went inside, down to the basement. Rickie Jay has a real barbershop, with the chair and everything in his basement. He even has the box with the blue light, where you put the clippers. I used to let him cut my hair until I learned how to do it myself. He got an attitude because of that. Like the five dollars he was getting from me was really doing his pockets that much more justice. He started back talking to me after a while, but I really didn't care if he did or not.   He's still an alright guy though. He just has some crazy mannerisms.

"Just give me an Even Steven," Mike noted.

While he was cutting, we just sat there chillin' and talking amongst ourselves until we heard Rickie Jay and Mike arguing.

"Man, put the money up."

"You ain't got no damn money. All you do is kill people for chump change. That ain't no real money," Rickie Jay yelled.

"Who you talking to like that, Dawg? Keep your voice down for real, Homie."

"Man don't get tough with me, cuz, you already know what time it is" Rickie Jay turned off the clippers and sat them down.

"Oh yeah, well what it is then, since you wanna' be tough?"

"DIS!" Rickie Jay pulled out a 357 and pointed it at Mike's head.

"Rickie Jay, watchu' doin', Dawg?" I yelled.

"Man, your boy killed my cousin and I ain't too happy about that."

"So, what, you gon' kill him?"

"You know how it is," he cocked the hammer back.

"Naw, chill out, Bird," Mike said. "Let's see how tough he really is." Mike remained cool, still sitting in the chair with the cape around him. "So, watcha' gonna' do, Homie? Pull the trigger or what?"

Rickie Jay was biting down on his bottom lip breathing hard.

"Yeah, I though s—"

Blagah!!

Before Mike could even finish his sentence he knocked the gun outta' Rickie Jay's hand just as he pulled the trigger. Now, they were on the ground wrestling. We all jumped up not knowing what to do because we didn't wanna' make any mistakes. Rickie Jay had managed to get loose and went straight for the gun. I didn't wanna' do it but I had no choice.

BhaLooGahh!!

Everybody stopped right in their movements.

"Bird, where you get that from?" Buck asked.

I knew he always kept it under the chair.

I had blown Rickie Jay's brains all over the basement with a 12 gauge. The barrel was still smoking and I still had it pointing at him like he wasn't already in the Heavens somewhere.

"Man, what the hell we gon' do now?" Mike asked.

"I don't know! You're the professional. What do you usually do with bodies afterwards?"

"We usually just leave it and go."

"We can't just leave him here," Gooney said paranoid.

"Well…" I tried to come up with a plan but nothing was registering. That was until I heard the garbage truck outside. It sounded like it was probably around the corner.

"I got it!" Ike yelled.

"What? What is it?" Mike asked.

"Let's cut him up and put the body in a bag."

"Then what?" Said Buck.

"Then we gone put him in the dumpster and let the garbage man put him in the truck." Ike explained.

Everyone was silent to Ike's suggestion. They were probably more willing to just leave the body lying on the floor.

"What ya'll looking around for? Let's cut up the body into pieces and throw them in a bag," Ike yelled.

I didn't wanna' do it myself, but I didn't want to risk getting caught and spending the rest of my life behind bars.

"This is how the Motor City Hitta's get down" Ike said coming downstairs with an ax in his hands and some kitchen knives in his pockets.

"Now that's what I'm talking about. At least somebody acting like they don't want to go to jail." Mike nodded his head liking the idea.

"This is foul man," Gooney said looking sick.

"So, who's gonna' make the first cut?" Buck asked.

We all looked at each other trying to figure out who was going to do it.

"Alright, well how about we pick a number from 1 to10," I suggested. "Whoever picks the number she has or closest to it goes first."

"Who gon' choose the number?" Mike asked.

"Gooney"

"Gooney! Why she get to choose the number?" Buck was pissed off.

"Cause she's a girl. Seems like being a girl paid off huh Gooney. You got a number in your head?"

She nodded.

"OK, Mike. Pick first."

"Why I gotta' pick first?"

"Okay. Well Buck, you pick first."

"Why I gotta' pi---"

"I'll pick first."

"Naw, I got it. Seven" Ike picked.

"Five" I yelled.

"Ten" Buck said.

"One" Mike said last.

"Gooney, what was it?"

"Five."

"Five," I yelled. "How the hell I pick the exact number?"

"Better you then anyone else bro. You the one who killed him," Buck said with relief.

I was pissed but I had to hurry if I wanted to catch the truck when it came around. I took a deep breath raising the ax in the air, closed my eyes, and came down hard. Gooney started throwing up as blood splattered everywhere. After I swung the first time I just kept choppin' away, not even thinking about it until the body was in pieces.

"Aight man, I did the hard part. Now ya'll gotta' put the body in the bag. We gotta' hurry too, cause the truck is coming down the street now."

They started putting the cut up pieces in the bag while I was wiping up blood from the floor, the walls, and all the furniture.

189

"What we gon' do with this?" Gooney pulled out the gauge.

"We taking it with us."

We stripped all off our clothes with blood on it down to our under clothes.

The body was in the bag so we hurried up the stairs to the back door, and threw the body in the dumpster. I rolled the dumpster to the curb just in time, because the truck was two houses down. I stood there waiting on the truck just to make sure it didn't skip. Everybody else stayed in the back and they all were paranoid. The garbage truck came over, picked up the dumpster, and dumped it into the back of the truck. Then, I rolled the dumpster back to the back of the house.

"So, what now?" Mike asked.

"We tell this to no one. You hear me? We don't even talk about this amongst ourselves. We family, right?" Everyone nodded. "We family, right?"

"Yeah, you know that, Bro."

"We taking this one to the grave, right?" Everyone nodded in agreement, and we all pinkie swore at the same time.

"Let's get outta' here, I'm starting to feel nauseous."

We jumped in the car and took off. Everyone was quiet. I knew we all were thinking the same thing. Gooney had started crying, so Mike wrapped his arms around her to console her.

My crew was solid, and I knew I could count on them. As long as everybody kept his or her word, we would be all right. I had no doubt in them, and I knew they didn't doubt me. It's a beautiful thing to have people around you that you can really call your friends. We'd been through a lot, but it was never anything this severe. How is God going to forgive me for this one? I'm hell bound for real now.

Life Starts When The Church Ends

CHAPTER 15

For a few months we didn't really do much at all. We were so scared that we were going to jail every time we heard people in the neighborhood talk about it. Even though we had gotten away with it, it still felt like we would be raided at any moment, and the SWAT team would come running outta' nowhere.

"Bird," I heard someone whispering. "Bird." I turned over and looked out the window. It was Gooney.

"What's up?"

"You sleep?"

"Nope, what's up?"

"I'm paranoid again. Is your mama home?"

"Naw, hold on. Go around to the front door."

I had been letting Gooney sleep in my room from time to time because she sometimes couldn't sleep at home. My mom is never really home during the daytime hours during the week. Even if she was, she wouldn't know Gooney is here because she'd be all drugged up.

"Man, it's cold outside," Gooney came in with her night clothes still on, and a blanket around her. This was like Gooney's second home, and when she came over she always made herself comfortable. "Ya'll got something to eat?"

"I think my mom cooked some pork chops or something. Go see. I'm tired, I'll be in the room."

I don't know the last time I been to my spot house. I really didn't have to go there often because everybody that was there was taking care of everything anyway. I was basically getting paid to do nothing. That's the American way, but I'm gonna' swing by there today for a just a lil' while.

I got up and took my clothes off so I could hop in the shower, then Gooney walked in.

"Ooops, my bad," she said spitting out some Kool-Aid.

"What? You act like you ain't never seen a naked man before."

"I haven't!"

"Get outta' here. You mean to tell me all those parties you dance at with all them boys that be all up in your face none of them ever stripped for you?"

"Nope," she said still looking down between my legs.

"Gooney."

"Oh, my bad. I'm sorry." She started walking out the room.

"Come here."

"What?"

"Come back in here."

She backed up and stood in the doorway, "Yessss."

"Come here, silly." I smiled as she slowly came towards me looking confused. I looked at her in the eyes, biting my lower lip. She walked up to me and I put my hands around her thin waist. She looked up in my eyes.

"Bird," she whispered.

"Yes"

"What are you doing?"

I didn't even answer. I just started kissing her on the lips. Softly, I placed kisses on her, and after a while she started kissing me back. I went to the right side of her neck and began to lick and suck as she let out slight moans.

"Bird" she moaned.

I stopped kissing and looked at her. I was in full erection poking her in her stomach. She looked down and her eyes lit up like a Christmas tree. I looked at her and then started leading her towards my bed. She started kissing me back as I laid her down on my bed. I pulled down her pajama shorts, and then her panties. Her eyes were closed and she was moaning, holding on to the sides of my twin bed.

Her precious jewel was so pretty, and it looked moist. For her to be a virgin, her monkey was fat as hell. I started licking her inner thigh, making my way upward as she hissed. My shaft was throbbing so hard; I didn't think I could get any harder. I reached over into my drawer and pulled out a condom.

"Let me," she said wanting to put it on me.

I gave her the golden wrapper and let her do her thing as I watched her strap me up so the party could get started. She was acting like she knew what she was doing. It was kind of weird though because we've been knowing each other for so long that we were damn near brother and sister. I had to get this image outta' my head though, because it was starting to mess up my erection.

"Is that right?"

I nodded my head and she laid back down.

"Don't hurt me."

"Don't worry about that, I will tell you this though, it's going to hurt at first but it'll get better as we go, and it will start to feel good.

"How you know?"

"Somebody told me."

She laid back down, closed her eyes, and I climbed on top of her. I spread her legs and she was already dripping wet. Both sides of her thighs were wet from her fountain of love leaking all over the place. I grabbed my manhood, and stuck just the head in.

"Ssssslow," she hissed in euphoric ecstasy.

I pulled out a little bit then put just the head in again.

"Aww" she yelped as I drove back in. I pulled out again and put just a little more head in.

"Ssslow,' she grabbed onto my back.

I left half of my shaft in her soul so she could get used to my presence. After a few seconds, I drove a little bit deeper and her nails dug into my back. She has me wanting to moan from the pain of her nails, but she was feeling too good for me to worry about that at this point.

All these years of me seeing her shake her butt around, and the certain amenities like the hips to go with it, and I'm now in the triple stage of the darkness within her soul. I dug in a lil' bit deeper, and after that I was just about all the way in. I pulled out slow, just halfway, and went back in even slower than the time before.

"Ooooooh," she moaned with her eyes closed and mouth wide open. "Hmm..."

My heart was beating a million miles an hour as I was softly stroking her. I could tell it was starting to feel good to her because she was no longer letting out sounds of pain. She was starting to feel good inside, as she pulled me tight around my waist with her legs, forcing me to go deeper.

"Hm... hm... hm... aw..." she moaned biting down on her bottom lip. By this time, I had a lil rhythm and was stroking slowly. In...and out...and...in...and out...

It started feeling so good I started playing around in it. I would go half way in for nine strokes, then all the way on the tenth stroke. "Hmph...hmph..." she moaned as I started rubbing up against her walls going side ways. I went in for eight strokes, then all the way in on the ninth stroke, giving her every inch of pleasure. I was displaying the true definition of wall to wall.

"Curtis," she moaned.

"Yes baby?"

"What?"

"You called me."

"No, I didn't."

"Cuuuurrrtis, I'm home." I heard my mom yell, and we both jumped up. Gooney was rushing to put her clothes on, and falling all over the place. I just threw my shorts on as my heart was about to jump through my chest.

"Curtis, where are you boy? Come here for a minute." My mom was calling me to the front room.

What am I gonna, do Bird?"

"Your guess is as good as mine."

I'm usually quick on my feet when it comes to decision-making, but this time I couldn't even think of anything but getting caught. I didn't even say a word back to my mom. I didn't know why, because I could hear her coming through the hallway towards my room. Once I heard her in front of the door knocking, my heart was damn near in my throat, and I swallowed it back down.

After two knocks she came right in, "Awww look at you two." Gooney was in my bed under the covers acting like she was sleep, and I was on the floor acting like I was sleep. We were both facing the opposite direction of the doorway.

"Uh…hm…hey mama" I said with a fake morning yawn, like I had been sleep for hours.

"Just wanted to let you know I was home. I haven't seen you in a while. I just wanted to talk. I'll let ya'll sleep."

"Hm-kay" I acted like I was wiping crust out the corner of my eyes. I was really getting my acting on by this point. My mom left out and closed the door.

"And the Oscar goes too," Gooney whispered.

"That was good. Wasn't it?"

We started laughing trying to keep quiet at the same time.

"What we doing today?" she asked.

"I don't know. Ike said he wanted to go to this Fourth of July party over at this park on Six Mile and Greenfield. You wanna' go?"

"You know it."

"Well, go home and get dressed. I'll come out in a few hours."

Gooney got up out the covers, and I looked at my sheets.

"Gooney," I whispered.

"What?"

"Look what you did to my sheets."

"Ooops," she put her hands over her mouth. "My bad," she started laughing.

"Go home, girl"

"Bye, boy."

"Ouch," she hit me in my piece before leaving out.

CHAPTER 16

AT THE PARK

We all linked up later on that evening. We were riding down Grand River towards the park Ike was talking about on Six Mile and Greenfield. Usually we smoke when we ride, but this day was unusual. It was a day unlike the rest, probably because we haven't been out like this since we cut up the body. None of us have mentioned it to one another. But I knew, just like they did, that it was still in the very front of the door of my memory. We made a pact though, and we honored it.

The weather is good for the most part, and it's a really good breeze floating in the air on this Fourth of July night. Different parking lots were jammed due to people getting ready to shoot off some fireworks.

"Hey man, I hope this park's jumpin'," I yelled to Ike.

"Don't worry about it, Dawg. Trust me, it's mad females over in this area."

"How you know?" his brother asked.

"Don't think we ain't always around, Bro. I get money on the side too you know. It's always a job to do over this way."

"So you going in the same neighborhood?"

"Naw naw. I ended up meeting a few females over here."

We pulled up to the park. It was nearly dusk outside. The sky was a mixture of dark orange and purple. They had a concert going on, and it looked like it was one of the local groups up there. They all had black leather coats, like letterman jackets that read "The Bottom" on them. They were probably the coldest group in Detroit. It's either them or the "Them Boyz." They stay beefin' though. That's probably why neither of them got a major record deal.

I swear, if all of Detroit rappers got together and stop hatin' on each other, we would be on the map. It's crazy to me, but that's how the Black Bottom or as we call it nowadays, the Dirty Mitten seems to be. We got outta' the car and stood around the area scoping out the scene. For the most part, it seemed like people were having a good time.

"Bird," I turned around and Gooney was calling me to the back of the car.

"What's up?"

"You can't tell anybody."

I started smiling "I'm not, I'm not."

"Watchu' smiling for?" she shoved me.

"I'm serious. I'm not gonna' tell anybody, but how am I going to explain that puddle you left in my sheets."

"Boy, shut up," she shoved me again as I laughed.

I hugged her and went back to the front of the car.

"Ya'll wanna' walk through the crowd," Mike suggested.

"Let's go!" We all agreed.

The crowd was hyped up listening to The Bottom on the ones and twos.

"Ooooh, you hear that," I yelled referring to the lyrics.

It was slappin' out here, and we were feeling it coming through throwing our hands in the air. We were dipping through the crowd, bobbin our heads. It felt good to be out again, and I have to admit, I was having many sleepless nights. When I did go to sleep, I was waking up in cold sweats.

My mom came in one night and she said she heard me hollering. When she came in my room, I was having a nightmare. I didn't tell any of the crew that, because I wanted to make it seem like it was effortless behind the curtains. I was just as upset at Gooney.

"Aye, look," Gooney pointed.

It was the same girls that were hatin' on her at that house party she shut down. We all looked at the same time giving them the stare down. They just rolled their eyes and acted like they didn't see us.

"Ah..ha..you mad…" Gooney said laughing at them as they walked to the other side of the park. There was a table open, so we went over and sat down.

"Check this out" Ike pulled out a chrome Glock 9.

"Dawg, where you get that from?" I jumped in excitement because those are my favorite brand of guns.

"I got it this morning from a base head. He only wanted a gram of heroin."

"Yeah, but you don't sell heroin", Buck chimed in.

"I know. I ran in the house and put a lil sugar in a lil piece of plastic and tied it tight," he laughed.

"Man, get the hell outta' here," I said in disbelief.

"Straight up, Homie."

"Man, you gotta let me get that, Dawg."

"Naw, I'm gonna' shoot it tonight once they start shooting off the fireworks."

"They about to do that now."

"I know, that's why I got it out. For real though man, I got this for you…Happy Birthday!"

"WHAT??" I was elated holding it in my hand. "Man, thank you dawg. Now, THIS is a birthday present." I pointed it straight forward with my right eye squinted low. My birthday is in a couple of hours, and it was the perfect time to shoot off my new gun. In a way, I didn't want to because I don't want to waste any bullets.

"I'm gonna' wait to shoot it."

"What? Man give me my gun back," Ike reached. "You gotta' shoot it off. It's your birthday."

"Yeah, boy, it's your birthday," Gooney said.

"Well, what you get me for my birthday then?"

"Oh, you forgot," she raised her eyebrow.

"Hmm. What ya'll got going on?" Mike asked.

I looked at Gooney and she looked the other way. We sat at the table throughout the night, chillin'. Buck went to the store and came back with some liquor, orange juice, and cush.

We just sipped away watching the fireworks show, and laughing at old memories that never get old.

As they went on and on about the past I drifted off into my own thoughts. It seemed like once I started getting into the streets, and stopped going to church, I'd been getting into a lot of trouble. Nothing that I couldn't handle, of course, but it just seemed like I'm at a point where I just might give God a try one more time. Although He has had my back since I was a kid, I guess it wouldn't hurt to show Him thanks by getting back spiritually rooted. I don't know why I stopped going anyway. Oh wait! Yes I do. This world made everything seem so good, and it sucked me right into its womb. I remember a saying that Jesus said and it's something like "Be in this world, but not of it." Clearly, I was both in the world and the world was me.

I looked at my crew as they were laughing and drinking, having a good time. I thought to myself, "If they weren't here, then who would be my friends." I didn't feel that there was anyone else that was remotely close to being as loyal as them. Then, I looked a bit deeper into the equation and asked myself the same questions again. Instead of answering it with my conscious mind, I dug into my subconscious.

If my friends weren't here, God would still be my friend. He always has, and will always be. I just find it hard to live the life that He wants me to live because I like doing the things that I do. I can't even believe that He is still staying by my side. Even though I'm sipping on the poison, He's still right here next to me.

"Come on, Bird."

"Huh…what?"

"It's almost midnight."

"Naw, I ain't gon' shoot it."

"What? Give it to me, I'll make it rain bullets out here." Ike reached around my waist trying to get it from me.

"Aight, aight, aight, ya'll ready?" I pulled it out and cocked the hammer. Ike was looking at his watch counting off the last few seconds til' midnight.

"3, 2" They all yelled simultaneously "1."

Blagah! Blagah! Blagah! Blagah!

"Oooh we!" Ike yelled. "That boy sounds good."

"Happy Birthday, Homie." Everyone came giving me fives and half shoulder hugs.

Gooney came and kissed me on the lips and squeezed my butt.

"Ugh...that's nasty," Buck said. "Bro, that's like your sister."

"Man, shut up," I pushed him.

"Aye, Homie, me and my brother about to walk over to these chicks' house. We'll holla at ya'll tomorrow. We good."

"Holla."

"Happy Birthday again, Boy." Ike and his brother gave me another five and a half shoulder hug. They left walking. Gooney, Buck and I headed to the car.

"Man, I am so hungry right now" I said. "Ya'll ain't' hungry?"

"Hell yeah. Let's ride around until we find something good." Buck shouted rubbing his stomach.

We were riding down Grand River looking for somewhere to get something to eat. I was so high that anything would have been good right about now.

"One of my homeboys from school works down at the White Castle on Lahser. He told me he'd be working tonight," I said.

"Well, let's go."

I drove down to the White Castle on Grand River and Lahser across the street from KFC and McDonalds. That's when it all went down.....

Whoop! Whoop! Whoop!

"Come on, Bird. Hurry up!"..."Don't move. Put your hand up"..."Two bodies, a robbery, and the possible murder weapon"..."You're going down tonight buddy"..."Man, I swear I didn't do anything"..."I done told you to stop running in those streets"..."Tim, I swear I d..."..."Well, deal with it"...

CHAPTER 17

MODERN DAY

COURT

So here I am, court day. All of my family is here, including Gooney and the rest of the crew. It was good to have some support to show the judge that I had a good team in back of me. The jury is still in the back trying to decide if I'm guilty or not. Buck and everyone else didn't find Tom Tom so it was my word against theirs. The only witness I had was Gooney and Buck, but that didn't help at all.

I knew I shouldn't have shot off the gun Ike gave me for my birthday. I should have just gone with my first mind. I couldn't even explain the gun powder on my hand because it was the same gun that was used in the robbery. The Italian from the store didn't even show up like he was supposed to, so I had to deal with the court appointed attorney, and he didn't give a damn whether I went to prison for the rest of my life or not. He was getting paid either way.

I've talked to God for hours before court and I hope He heard my plea. I even promised Him that I'll leave here and do whatever He wanted me to do if He got me outta' this mess. I even went on a three day fast with no food or water. I mean, I couldn't have pleaded any more than that. I should pray again right now just to send Him another voicemail via air.

I looked over at my mom and I could tell she was ready to burst out and cry again. My grandmother was rubbing her back trying to console her. I looked at Gooney and she was rubbing her stomach. She finally told me that she is pregnant with our baby. The news was bittersweet because I'm in a position where I could never spend any time with her or with the baby.

"Dear God, if you're listening this time, I swear, if you just get me out of this situation right here I will live a saved, sanctified life. I don't want to be a part of the streets again. I'm ready to come back home. I'll even stop listening to rap CDs just to show you that I'm serious. God, if you're listening, please let me live with my new family. I mean you wouldn't want my son growing up without a father would you? Or what if it's a girl? You wouldn't want her without her daddy's advice would you? Please, if you could just hear me. I'm ready God...I'm ready..." A tear came rolling down my cheek.

I didn't bother looking at my mother so she couldn't see I was crying, so I put my head down instead.

"All rise," the officer said.

The judge came in with the jury, and it looked like he was pissed off. We all sat down and before the judge said anything he just looked at me all crazy.

"Did you really think that you had a chance of winning this case? You had the audacity to come up in my court room and thought you were going to get away like that? Killing two people and robbing the place, you thought justice wasn't going to be served for that? Well, I guess you thought wrong."

The judge was talking real nasty to me, and my mom just busted out crying all over the place. Gooney followed right behind her, crying as well. I just know the judge is about to railroad me, but it's not even up to him. It's up to the jury but he's making them feel like I should be found guilty.

"Jury, do we have a verdict?" the judge asked.

"Yes, sir. We do."

"May we hear it?"

One person from the jury stood up with some paper in his and walked toward the mic.

"Hm mph." He cleared his throat. "When it comes to the case of Curtis Marcel Books we the jury find the defendant G……"

"WAAAIITTT!" Someone yelled busting through the door.

It was the Italian and a little girl.

"Order in the court," the judge slammed down the gavel. "Order!"

Everyone was looking confused, including me. My mom and Gooney came back in the courtroom, and the Italian started walking down the aisle with the girl by his side.

"Your honor, this girl has the only evidence that will free this boy right now."

"Let him through" the judge ordered. "And what do you have?" he asked.

"A cell phone, your honor, this little girl was playing with her mother's cell phone while they were waiting on their food at White Castle. The phone has a video recorder on it, and she happened to record the whole thing. She thought she was taking pictures of her mom but she was recording. Look." He took the phone to the judge and showed it to him.

The judge watched it, and his jaw dropped like he didn't have a muscle in it to hold it up.

The Italian turned towards me and winked. I was sitting at the edge of my chair waiting on what was about to happen next. He watched the whole video, and then gave the phone back to the Italian. He grabbed his gavel and banged it three times.

"Order!" he yelled. Everyone was confused about what was taking place.

"After reviewing the only evidence that we have, I have no choice but to find this man innocent of all charges. Someone take the cuffs off him. This court is adjourned." He slammed the gavel down.

All of my family and friends were hoopin' and hollerin' like crazy. Gooney ran up to me and started kissing me, hugging me all around my neck. I couldn't even explain how I was feeling at that moment. It was the best natural high I had ever experienced. I looked up at the Heavens and said, "I won't let you down, I promise. Thank you, God."

EPILOGUE

It's been about a month and a half since the charges were dropped, and it's such a relief. That Italian really came through. He did want me to work for him, but I started telling him about my reconnection with God, and how I owed my life to Him. He understood, and let me do me. It feels good to be back in church now. I even caught the Holy Ghost a few times since I've been back. My energy was so high that I couldn't even stand it any longer, and I just started jumping all around, like crazy. I was damn near doing the stanky leg at one point. I had to catch myself.

Life has been a lot easier though, and I don't think it could get any better than what it is. God has blessed me with good grades in school, and allowed me to leave the past in the past. I know He forgave me for what happened in my history, and I don't have any regrets. I figured that I had to go through those things just so I could be made over. Nobody could go through what I did and that's a blessing in itself that God chose me of all people to suffer so much just because He really loved me. Tough love I guess, but I ain't trippin'.

I'm getting baptized today for the second time. The first time was when I was younger down south. It was time to fully wash away the old me and be made over. My mom was there with the video recorder, and she's even been coming to church on the regular also, she told me she was doing a lot of praying and fasting while I was locked up. I don't think she's even missed a bible study either. It was good that she had gotten herself together.

"You ready?" my mom asked smiling.

"Yeah."

"I'm so proud of you," she kissed me on the cheek.

Usually when she tells me that I would ask her why. She would just smile and say "just because you're my son, and you're the chosen one." When I think of that though, it weirds me out. My mom couldn't have any more kids after me. What if she did? My younger brother or sister would have been trying to follow behind me, and something awful could have happened. God knew this and allowed my mom to have only one child, and it was me, 'The Chosen One'.

"Curtis Marcel Books" the pastor yelled for me to come to the water next. The church was singing an old hymn "take me to the water…"

I walked down the middle isle on some plastic they laid down so the carpet wouldn't get wet. I had on all white from head to toe. I even had on white socks. Slowly, I walked towards the baptismal pool, I was moving from the past and was blessed to have a better future. This would put the icing on the cake right here. I walked up to the pool and into the water. It was cold so I stepped in real slow, putting one foot in at a time. There was the pastor greeting me as I got in. There was a deacon to the left. I walked all the way in, and the deacon held the microphone up to the pastor's mouth.

"This is a beautiful day in the Lord's sight"

"Yes sir," someone yelled.

"We are here to baptize this young man with in the name of the Father, the Son, and the Holy Ghost. The Bible says, "Train up a child in the way he should go, so when he gets old he won't depart from it." In the book of Revelations it says "and behold, all things are made new." I'm telling you we are bringing forth a new man in the eyes of the Lord today but I want to speak briefly to our young men in here for there is quite a few. Young men we have to do better. We have to not allow ourselves to be so impressionable. We see other males and it may look like his life is so much better than yours and we immediately gravitate to that. We forget that we have to fully develop into what we are destined to be. I believe we cheat God too much. We cheat God because we want to speed up the process of evolving. We want to take the easy route. We wanna' be noticed all the time. We want people especially women to look at us like we have everything together on the outside but on the inside we are savages. The bible says "Be aware of wolves in sheep clothing." If you think about it, we will ask a woman what she looks for in a man, right? Then once we know that, we pretend to be that person for a while. The woman, after a while finds out who we really are and questions us how much we changed. Wolves in sheep's clothing. A sheep goes through a shedding process and if you are a wolf, at some point after enough shedding you will began to reveal your real self. We waste our women time in trying to get in relationships and we know that we are only out for one thing. I'm just gonna' tell it like it is. If you can barely take care of yourself what makes you think you can be in a relationship? See, we are chasing the wrong things. We spend all this money on clothes, shoes, cars, and belts to impress women who only pay ten dollars for leggings. Ladies don't give me the side eye. You know I'm telling the truth. Again, men we are chasing the wrong things. We read more post and status on social media but we won't read a paragraph in the daily newspaper. Now, I'm not trying to sound like I'm perfect by any means because at one time in my life I was chasing the wrong things as well. What I did to change that around was allow God to be God and when you do that you start to evolve and certain things you were chasing becomes obsolete. You become wise. You begin to realize that you can either spend two hundred dollars for a dress shirt or you can go to the Salvation Army and pay two dollars for it because some wealthy man didn't want to throw it away. He decided to donate it so he can write it off at the end of the year and get the money back in his tax return only to use that money to buy new shirts. I know I'm saying something in here. I just want my young men to wise up and stop chasing the wrong things."

"You tell it, Preacher!"

He put his hands over my nose and mouth. "It's with the Father, the Son, and the Holy Ghost" he quickly dipped me in the water and pulled me out just as fast.

"Thannnnk yoooou, Jeeesussss!" I yelled when I came out. "Thank you merciful Father. Holy is your name among us oh precious Lord Jesus. Thank ya!" I was excited and in total bliss. I stepped outta the pool, and walked down the aisle as my mom was recording me. She had a tear coming down her cheeks, and so did I because she was happy. It's been a long time since I've really seen my mother happy, and I ran over to her and kissed her on the cheek. I walked back in the back room to dry off and change my clothes.

When I came back, service was just about over. I was feeling good on the inside like a completely new man. I looked out the window and people were doing the same ole thing. When I was younger the streets had intrigued me so much that I wanted to know 'why?' Once I realized that the streets had nothing to offer, I was wondering when everyone else would figure out the same thing. I guess that's why the scripture says that many are called, but only few are chosen.

"Curtis"

I turned around and it was my mother. "What's up, Ma?" I kissed her on the cheek.

"You coming downstairs to get something to eat?"

"Yeah, I'll be down there in a minute."

"Okay, well imma fix you a plate."

"Aight, Momma."

I turned around looking back out the window. "I know that ain't, it is…" I ran outside because Gooney and Buck, Mike and Ike were outside in the car.

"Man, ya'll are late," I yelled. I wasn't mad though because I was happy they came. The look on their faces was dull, and they looked angry.

"What's up, with ya'll?"

"Tom Tom."

"Tom Tom?"

"Yeah, we know here he is right now," Ike pulled out a gun. "It's fully loaded man."

My heart dropped to my knees, and I almost passed out. Lord knows how bad I wanted to see him after all that went down. I turned around and looked back at the church, and then back at them. It shouldn't even be a question or that hard of a decision. I'm a new man now, or so I thought.

I thought all the way back to what Uncle Charlie used to tell me. "Life starts when the church ends," and it just registered to me what he meant by that. The life is the reality of this world. Yeah, we come to church, and when we're in church we get so emotional that we forget what the real problems in life like bills, relationships, the streets, getting robbed, or killed for nothing. It's all safe in the church when you're crying and jumping all around having a good time, but when church is over, then what? It's back to reality. It's back to the real world, something that's not a fairytale, and strictly beyond being fiction.

"Let's ride!" I yelled getting in the car taking the gun from Ike. "I guess life starts when the church ends ya'll....hold on wait hold up. I told them as I opened the door and got out. I walked to the stairs of the church and turned and faced them. I can't do this. I......."

"CURTISSS!!!!" Gooney yelled.

I looked up and a black truck pulled up with the windows down and guns pointed at me.

"Remember, Ricky Jay, cuz?" they asked before pulling the trigger letting a thunder of bullets hit me in the chest. It felt like every bullet they spat out connected with my body.

I laid there and all I could see or think about was Jesus. He's done so much for me and I finally gave my life over to him. Like they say "You live by the gun; You die by the gun." It pays to have a good name and to be a person of good character. People will always be willing to help out and support someone who is making an effort to be a positive being on this earth. The moment your character diminishes so shall your life began to deteriorate.

God is indeed a forgiving God but when we make a promise to Him and He delivers us from the havoc we are having. We ignore Him as soon as we're out of trouble. We then create more problems than we were in. They say it's good to talk to God even when you don't want anything and I just remembered that I never spoke to Him unless I needed Him for something. I now understand that I never had a real personal relationship with God. I just depended on Him for my benefit

227

and that's pretty much a slap in the face. I didn't love God. I only loved Him for what He could do for me and He's revealing it to me right now as I lay here in need of Him again. Even when we fall short in being one with God He still comes to check on his children. What a mighty God we serve.

I was trying to catch my breath but was suffocating at the same time and Just before I took my next breath I saw my mom standing over and I whispered "Mom, I'm sor….."

AUTHORS NOTE

I want to thank everyone for reading. I hope you enjoyed this story as much as I enjoyed writing it. It has been a journey if you know my personal life but I am nevertheless moving and progressing forward doing the things I love. I just wanted to give you a brief story on how this book came about. I was telling a friend of mine by the name of Michigan Mike about my book idea. Michigan Mike was very intelligent in my opinion. He was a reader of many books and he understood the process of maturation really well. In fact, he is the one who taught me about the process of maturation. I told him about the title I had for this project which was "God's Disciple by day and Devils Angel by night." He said he didn't like the title because it would create possible controversy and by me being a new author It wouldn't be a wise thing to do. I listened and he gave me this title "Life Starts When The Church Ends" and said make the main character a young boy who's unlike his peers. Someone such as yourself. Some evolve a lot earlier than others and some like you, takes a little time. The process of maturation is never ending. It begins when we start to recognize the knowledge of self. I listened and then Bird was born.

Well, Michigan Mike isn't here to see the finished product because he was found gunned down next to his car when he came home from prison. I know if he was here, he would be proud of the messages that I presented while writing this book. He asked me a question at a round table and it stuck with me for a while and I want to leave you with the same thing. He said "Men can not only re-produce through just women but also other men. Can you tell me how?"

If you see me in public or on social media I want to hear your answers. Thank you and rest in peace Michigan Mike.

Sherrad O'Neil Glosson

www.ingramcontent.com/pod-product-compliance
Lightning Source LLC
Chambersburg PA
CBHW032117040426
42449CB00005B/168